"Each one of us has unique gifts or talents. And, most of our lives will be easier and happier if we make the most of those. Also, don't worry so much about what others think of you. Do what you think is right, and you'll be just fine!!!"

Most wonderful of all you have,
Je ne sais quoi... me

Before you can even think about bringing a supervillain to justice or thwarting the doomsday plot of a megalomaniacal industrialist, you must learn to master your powers. Impressive as your raw abilities may seem to you, chances are you haven't even scratched the surface of your true potential. By earnestly and compulsively applying yourself to the principles and exercises found in this book, you'll learn:

- How to identify which (or which combination) of the nine internationally recognized Power Classes you possess

- How to fully develop and hone your power(s) for maximum justice-distribution and evil-vanquishing effectiveness

- How to maintain a positive body image and healthy inner balance

- How to recognize the unique and often subtle characteristics that distinguish each power type from the next, as well as each one's unusual side effects and little-known weaknesses

How to Be a
SUPERHERO

**YOUR COMPLETE
GUIDE TO
FINDING A SECRET HQ,
HIRING A SIDEKICK,
THWARTING THE FORCES OF EVIL,
AND MUCH MORE!!**

BY

DOCTOR METROPOLIS

A PLUME BOOK

PLUME
Published by the Penguin Group
Penguin Group (USA) Inc., 375 Hudson Street, New York, New York 10014, U.S.A.
Penguin Group (Canada), 10 Alcorn Avenue, Toronto, Ontario, Canada M4V 3B2 (a division of
Pearson Penguin Canada Inc.)
Penguin Books Ltd, 80 Strand, London WC2R 0RL, England
Penguin Ireland, 25 St Stephen's Green, Dublin 2, Ireland (a division of Penguin Books Ltd)
Penguin Group (Australia), 250 Camberwell Road, Camberwell, Victoria 3124, Australia (a division
of Pearson Australia Group Pty Ltd)
Penguin Books India Pvt Ltd, 11 Community Centre, Panchsheel Park, New Delhi – 110 017, India
Penguin Books (NZ), Cnr Airborne and Rosedale Roads, Albany, Auckland, New Zealand
(a division of Pearson New Zealand Ltd)
Penguin Books (South Africa) (Pty) Ltd, 24 Sturdee Avenue, Rosebank, Johannesburg 2196,
South Africa

Penguin Books Ltd, Registered Offices: 80 Strand, London WC2R 0RL, England

First published by Plume, a member of Penguin Group (USA) Inc.

First Printing, December 2004
10 9 8 7 6 5 4 3 2 1

Copyright © Barret Neville, 2004
All rights reserved

℗ REGISTERED TRADEMARK—MARCA REGISTRADA

LIBRARY OF CONGRESS CATALOGING-IN-PUBLICATION DATA

Dr. Metropolis.
    How to be a superhero : your complete guide to finding a secret HQ, hiring a sidekick,
thwarting the forces of evil, and much more! / Dr. Metropolis ; [illustrated by] Luis Roca.
        p. cm
    ISBN 0-452-28575-5 (pbk.)
        1. Heroes — Humor.   I. Title.

PN6165.D7 2004
818'.607 — dc22   2004053515

Printed in the United States of America
Set in Adobe Garamond
Designed by Daniel Lagin

Contents

Special Bonus Chapter
On the Other Hand, Maybe You're Evil 183

Acknowledgments

For Sergeant Strong, Ultra-Sonik, and the Metro-Gnome: I couldn't have done it without you guys. A big round of applause for Nitro-Lad, the world's finest research assistant and fact-checker. My eternal gratitude to Gary Brozek, my editor, for believing in the project (and sorry again about that mix-up with the Iron Pharaoh!). Thanks also go out to the Colossal Skull and Where-Wolf for helping with the last chapter. And special thanks to the staffs of the Library of Congress, the Mister Mindmaster Library at New York University, and the Manhattan Project Historical Society.

Final thanks go to my sidekick, Stumbly. With you by my side, there's no tall building I can't leap.

How to Be a

SUPERHERO

Introduction

Awakening the Superhero Within

Each year, thanks to freak industrial accidents and top-secret experiments, thousands of people all over the world receive exciting new powers. *Super* powers. At the same time, however, they get little or no guidance in how to use these special abilities to become superheroes. If you believe you're one of these people, then this book is for you.

I wrote it because, though I've touched the lives of, literally, tens of thousands of promising crimefighters through my private coaching, weekend retreats, and five-disc audio programs, I felt I still had more to give. This book, the culmination of years spent helping bright, talented people reach their full superheroic potential, contains practical insights into every aspect of the superheroic development process, from honing your powers to designing your costume to choosing an arch-enemy.

Though I'm now a leading superhero coach and motivational speaker, it seems like only yesterday that I was bombarded by "dark moon" rays that gave me strange new powers. I can still remember my first night patrol. I didn't even have a proper costume then—just some polyester tights and a vicious case of mask itch. To make matters worse, I was calling myself "Johnny Atlas," a name that a copywriter friend had come up with.

It was just as I was preparing to leap to another rooftop that I suddenly found myself facing the superpowered criminal known as the Atomic Anarchist. I still remember him hovering over me, eyes blazing with wicked glee and a lethal charge of radiation. He was fast, much faster than I expected. Watching his fists begin to glow with a powerful radium current, it suddenly occurred to me that I didn't have the slightest idea what I was doing.

Though I somehow survived that battle, and went on to build a successful career as a superpowered crimefighter, I continued to suffer from debilitating feelings of inadequacy and self-doubt. These negative emotions sapped my confidence and self-esteem, and became so intolerable that I even considered retiring. But then one day, fed up with being depressed and miserable, I decided to share my problems with a fellow superhero.

I soon found out that I wasn't alone. Not only were most other superheroes hounded by the same misgivings, but they were also wrestling with guilt, shame, and questions like:

- "Am I just a freak?"
- "Will thwarting this fiendish plot really make a difference?"
- "Is it wrong to have feelings for Space Vixen?"

Why, I wondered, are we superheroes so prone to self-destructive thinking? I came to believe that the answer lay in the fact that most of us are left to fend for ourselves after receiving our secret powers. With no one to guide us on the path to becoming a superhero, it's all too easy to fall into hurtful patterns of negativity and low self-esteem.

The program I've outlined in this book is designed to work for anyone. It makes no difference whether you've been bitten by a radioactive spider or injected with a super-soldier serum. It doesn't matter if you're the last survivor of an alien race, or simply fell into a vat of mysterious Chemical X. Even if your powers come from something as simple as an advanced exo-battlesuit, or a ring entrusted to you by a dying alien, this book can help. Think of it as the owner's manual that should have come with your new powers.

So what will you learn in the next thirteen chapters? Well, you'll learn that you're not alone (even if it sometimes *feels* that way). You'll learn to appreciate, and even cherish, your new superpowers. You'll learn to love yourself for who you are, even if the rest of the world fears and/or hates you. And you'll learn how to get even tough stains, like blood, viscera, and Destruct-o-beam™ coolant, out of your costume.

But most of all, you'll learn to embrace your destiny and become . . . a SUPERHERO.

Unlike other so-called superhero self-help gurus, the program I've developed is designed to grow with you, helping you go from ordinary to extraordinary in thirteen easy-to-follow chapters. You've tried all those other hard-to-follow systems and expensive "special" programs—now try the one that *really* works.

What's so special about my approach? Well, it's the only one endorsed by the International Brotherhood of Superheroes

(IBSH) as well as the Benevolent Association of Professional Aides to the Superpowered Industry (also known as Sidekicks United!). Just follow my exclusive, step-by-step program and you'll learn how to:

- Navigate the crowded superhero real-estate market
- Master basic supervillain fighting techniques
- Hone your abilities using my superpower development program—it's guaranteed to work, and it covers all nine major powers!
- Double your sidekick's effectiveness as a supervillain hostage and comic foil
- Survive the ups and downs of the tumultuous archenemy relationship
- Develop your heroic persona, design a costume, craft a memorable origin story, and more!

But this book is not only for those who have been unexpectedly drenched with superpowers and are seeking to become fully licensed and accredited superheroes. The fact is, I often meet people who say to me, "Doctor Metropolis, I don't have any powers, but I want to be a superhero. What can I do?" If this sounds familiar, don't despair; this book is for you, too. Experts tell us that over the next ten years the two fastest-growing industries will be superheroics and health care. In fact, our industry is experiencing such explosive growth that even superheroes whose abilities are of questionable value in the ongoing struggle against petulance—such as the Stare-Master—have become the objects of bidding wars between municipalities in need of heroes.

In fact, because this exciting and fast-growing field is experiencing such unprecedented demand, all kinds of opportunities are appearing that didn't even exist a few years ago. For instance, more entry-level sidekick positions are available now than ever before, with more being created each day. Sidekicking is an excellent way to break into the business, and the good news is, superpowers aren't always necessary. In fact, the two qualities that the majority of superheroes say they look for in a sidekick are enthusiasm and the willingness to sign a waiver.

In addition to sidekicking, you can also apply for an internship with one of the more established super-teams, justice leagues, or superheroic legions. Now, I won't lie to you: part of being an intern means getting coffee and picking up capes from the dry cleaner. But working so closely with superheroes also means you'll have plenty of opportunities to become exposed to all kinds of strange chemicals, harmful radiation, and mysterious energy fields. If you were to "accidentally" wander through the stream of a high-frequency neutronic ray, for instance, who knows what kind of fabulous superpowers might result? Assuming, of course, that you survive.

My work as a teacher and coach means I'm on the road a lot, and my travels often bring me into contact with people who want to acquire superpowers in order to compensate for some part of their lives with which they're unhappy. If this sounds familiar, then good for you! I'm a firm believer in the idea that people can solve their problems by exposing themselves to dangerous chemicals, untested secret formulas, and massive doses of radiation.

The good news is, there's a whole world of opportunity out there, a world filled with poorly maintained toxic-waste dumps, leaky nuclear-power plants, and unscrupulous scientists willing to experiment on anyone they can get their hands on. So what are you waiting for? Your future, a *super* future, awaits!

ACING THE SAT (SUPERHERO APTITUDE TEST)

Before turning to Chapter One, I strongly recommend that you take a moment to complete the following SAT, or Superhero Aptitude Test. Make sure you're well rested and have eaten a hearty breakfast before attempting to take the SAT. You'll also need two sharp Number 2 pencils and a quiet place where you'll be able to concentrate without distractions. And remember, all your work should be your own. If you're even thinking about cheating, then you're most likely a supervillain and should turn immediately to the special Bonus Chapter, "On the Other Hand, Maybe You're Evil."

Remember, there are no wrong answers, only wrong, twisted, deeply depraved people.

SAT (SUPERHERO APTITUDE TEST)

1. **I have the ability to fly.**

    ☐ Strongly disagree   ☐ Somewhat disagree   ☐ No opinion
    ☐ Somewhat agree   ☐ Strongly agree

2. **I often find myself battling evil geniuses who are bent on world domination.**

    ☐ Strongly disagree   ☐ Somewhat disagree   ☐ No opinion
    ☐ Somewhat agree   ☐ Strongly agree

3. **I feel that when our forefathers composed the Second Amendment to the United States Constitution, they couldn't possibly have been thinking about things like freeze rays.**

    ☐ Strongly disagree   ☐ Somewhat disagree   ☐ No opinion
    ☐ Somewhat agree   ☐ Strongly agree

4. **I think that if we want real justice in this country, we should take authority away from police officers, lawyers, judges, courts, and impartial juries, and give it to people who wear capes and booties.**

    ☐ Strongly disagree   ☐ Somewhat disagree   ☐ No opinion
    ☐ Somewhat agree   ☐ Strongly agree

5. **I have fallen into a vat of Chemical X in the past three months.**

    ☐ Strongly disagree   ☐ Somewhat disagree   ☐ No opinion
    ☐ Somewhat agree   ☐ Strongly agree

6. **I can bench-press eight million times my own body weight.**

    ☐ Strongly disagree   ☐ Somewhat disagree   ☐ No opinion
            ☐ Somewhat agree   ☐ Strongly agree

7. **I have been known to project Destruct-o-beams from my eyes.**

    ☐ Strongly disagree   ☐ Somewhat disagree   ☐ No opinion
            ☐ Somewhat agree   ☐ Strongly agree

8. **At some point in the past month I have been bitten by a radioactive spider.**

    ☐ Strongly disagree   ☐ Somewhat disagree   ☐ No opinion
            ☐ Somewhat agree   ☐ Strongly agree

9. **I come from a faraway planet that orbits a red sun.**

    ☐ Strongly disagree   ☐ Somewhat disagree   ☐ No opinion
            ☐ Somewhat agree   ☐ Strongly agree

10. **When I grow angry, I tend to become a kind of emerald-hued man-child, with fantastic strength and a proclivity for flattening buildings, smashing cars, and generally disturbing the peace, and yet I never seem to harm anyone.**

    ☐ Strongly disagree   ☐ Somewhat disagree   ☐ No opinion
            ☐ Somewhat agree   ☐ Strongly agree

11. **I enjoy tying a towel around my neck, pretending it's a cape, and running around my house.**

    ☐ Strongly disagree   ☐ Somewhat disagree   ☐ No opinion
            ☐ Somewhat agree   ☐ Strongly agree

12. **(If you strongly agree with the above statement) I also stick my arms out in front of me while making a "swooshing" sound.**

   ☐ Strongly disagree   ☐ Somewhat disagree   ☐ No opinion
         ☐ Somewhat agree   ☐ Strongly agree

13. **I have been bombarded by gamma rays at least once in the past twelve months.**

   ☐ Strongly disagree   ☐ Somewhat disagree   ☐ No opinion
         ☐ Somewhat agree   ☐ Strongly agree

14. **I frequently find that I can move objects, such as the state of Nebraska, with my mind.**

   ☐ Strongly disagree   ☐ Somewhat disagree   ☐ No opinion
         ☐ Somewhat agree   ☐ Strongly agree

15. **I am the incarnation of a mythical god or goddess.**

   ☐ Strongly disagree   ☐ Somewhat disagree   ☐ No opinion
         ☐ Somewhat agree   ☐ Strongly agree

16. **I enjoy wearing tight, revealing clothes.**

   ☐ Strongly disagree   ☐ Somewhat disagree   ☐ No opinion
         ☐ Somewhat agree   ☐ Strongly agree

17. **I am currently in possession of a mystical artifact that gives me great and terrifying powers.**

   ☐ Strongly disagree   ☐ Somewhat disagree   ☐ No opinion
         ☐ Somewhat agree   ☐ Strongly agree

18. **I have recently (in the last two years) escaped from a top-secret government research facility somewhere in the Rocky Mountains, where I was the subject of numerous and indescribably painful genetic tests that violated me in every significant way.**

☐ Strongly disagree   ☐ Somewhat disagree   ☐ No opinion
☐ Somewhat agree   ☐ Strongly agree

19. **I often find myself being pursued by shadowy government forces.**

☐ Strongly disagree   ☐ Somewhat disagree   ☐ No opinion
☐ Somewhat agree   ☐ Strongly agree

Evaluating Your Score

To calculate your score, first assign each of your answers a numerical equivalent:

Strongly agree = 5
Somewhat agree = 4
No opinion = 3
Somewhat disagree = 2
Strongly disagree = 1

Now, add up your score and rate your superhero potential according to the key below:

90–73: You have great power, and with great power comes a dizzying array of legally binding obligations and promotional commitments.

72–53: You'll make a fine addition to any of our more prominent super-teams.

52–37: You may want to start with some white-collar crime before calling out Doctor Ominous.

36–18: Sidekicking is a noble part of the superhero tradition.

Part One

Getting to Know Your Superpower

"I truly believe that inside each of us is this extraordinary person, and to release him or her we need only have the good fortune to get caught in a potentially disfiguring and almost certainly lethal industrial accident."
—Doctor Metropolis

As part of my job, I'm privileged to have the opportunity to work with young people from all over the country who are interested in becoming superheroes. I listen, constantly humbled and inspired by their heroic spirit, as they tell amazing stories of attempting to acquire superpowers by sneaking onto nuclear test ranges or eagerly injecting themselves with various untested formulas and controlled substances. At the same time, however, I can't help but chuckle condescendingly when I hear them say things like, "Once I get my powers, then I'll be a real superhero!" or "As soon as I have my secret origin, then all my problems will be solved!"

If only life were that simple.

Before you can even think about bringing a supervillain to justice or thwarting the doomsday plot of a megalomaniacal industrialist, you must learn to master your powers. Impressive as your raw abilities may seem, chances are you haven't even scratched the surface of your true potential. Only by earnestly and compulsively applying yourself to the principles and exercises found in this section will you learn:

- How to identify which (or which combination) of the eight internationally recognized power classes you belong to[1]
- How to fully develop and hone your power(s) for maximum justice-distribution and evil-vanquishing effectiveness
- How to maintain a positive body image and healthy inner balance
- How to recognize the unique and often subtle characteristics that distinguish each power type from the next, as well as each one's unusual side effects and little-known weaknesses

As you struggle through this section, you'll discover that along with the description of each power type, I've prescribed a series of simple exercises designed to help you mold and shape your special talents into an arsenal of vengeful goodness. Unlike other books and programs that insist on a "one-size-fits-all" approach, my system is specifically calibrated to the dis- tinctive limits and requirements of your unique power combination.

In fact, the harder you work at the program, the more you'll begin to notice *real* improvements, not only in your ability to use your powers but also in your ability to *get more out of life.*

---

1. As of this writing, I've done my best to cover all major classes of meta-human ability currently recognized by the BMHA. However, as we continue to make advances into the field of meta-human study, new classifications are emerging all the time. If for some reason you don't see your specific ability represented here, please e-mail me at drmetropolis84@yahoo.com and, if appropriate, I'll be sure to include your power in later editions.

For example, after just a few sessions you may find that not only has your cruising speed almost doubled, but you also feel more energetic and alert. You notice that while outrunning bullets, you're also shedding unwanted pounds. Once-agonizing physical transformations may become painless and routine. Meanwhile, your skin is clearer, and you feel more confident with each passing day.*

What's more, my program can be performed in the privacy of your own home, using as little specialized equipment as possible. While old "superpower" development programs relied on fancy equipment and unreliable "danger rooms" that could cost millions of dollars and take months to work, my system allows you to develop complete mastery over your meta-abilities in less than half the time and at a fraction of the cost. And with only twenty minutes of honing a day, three to four days a week, you'll start to see results in less than a month!

YOU CAN'T FIGHT EVIL
WHILE FIGHTING A COLD

Before beginning any new superpower training or development program, the first thing you need to do is to see your family doctor or a well-referred general practitioner. He or she will help you make sure that you're physically prepared for the rigors of a superheroic career. Some of the questions your doctor will probably ask you include:

---

*Editor's Note: Your actual experience may vary wildly. For best results, program should be augmented by a steady diet of morphine, Oil of Olay, and antidepressants.

- Do you have any history of heart problems in your family?
- Did you suffer from any illnesses as a child? Asthma, for example? Or scurvy?
- Do you have any trouble seeing through certain kinds of metal?
- Any unexplained aches or pains? Frequent headaches?
- Any sensitivity to kryptonite? What about red kryptonite?
- Do certain colors make you feel weak or disoriented?
- Ho much sleep would you say you usually get in a week?
- Do you smoke? If so, is that before or after activating your geothermal powers?
- Have you noticed any tenderness around your lymph nodes? And what about your wings? Any unusual molting or lice?

HELPFUL HINT ALERT!
Remember: any hero operating without full medical clearance is not an agent of justice, but a dangerous menace—to himself, his teammates, and the citizens who look to him for protection.

- Are you currently on any other medication? Any other secret formulas, experimental serums, anything like that?
- Have you had unprotected sex in the past year?
- Do you use IV drugs? When injecting yourself with mysterious chemicals, do you share needles with other superheroes or supervillains?
- Noticed any invulnerability lately? Bullets bouncing off your skin, for example?
- Anyone in your family with mutant abilities? Maybe an uncle who could read minds or a cousin who could walk through walls?

- How's your vision been? Any problems driving at night? Noticed any heat rays or optic blasts painfully extruding from your eyes?

PREPARING YOUR BODY FOR A SUPER-WORKOUT

You should always perform a few warm-up exercises before attempting any type of superpowered activity. This is particularly important when you're honing your powers for the first time. Just ten minutes of basic heroic warm-ups can help you avoid serious injury or impairment of your powers. As you'll see, the following warm-up routine is specially formulated for superheroes. In fact, it's the same one I use before patrolling or setting out to confront a supervillain. Count on it to help ward off painful sprains, muscle pulls, and spontaneous limb detachments.

> "Take care of your powers and your powers will take care of you!"
> —Anonymous

Heroic Locust Pose

Step 1: Stand with your feet shoulder-width apart. Your knees should be relaxed and your hands clenched in tight clumps of wrath.

Step 2: Keeping your pelvis tucked and your chin level, slowly lift your arms until your upper arms are level with your shoulders.

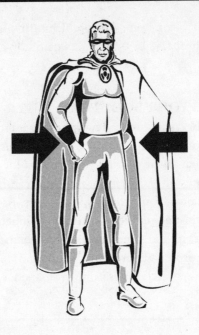

Figure 1-1

Step 3: Now, slowly lower your arms while simultaneously pulling your fists inward until they come to rest on your hips (see *Figure 1-1*). (Note: You may also rest them on your waist.)

Step 4: Repeat until your chest becomes bloated with either pride or heroic energy.

Hysterical Tiger Pose

Step 1: Stand with your feet shoulder-width apart. Relax your knees while keeping your upper body somewhat schlumpy.

Step 2: Being careful to keep your weight on your heels, release your knees and ankles, and collapse to a kneeling position.

Step 3: While keeping your shoulders relaxed, tilt your head back. Pivot your arms away from your body slightly and arrange your hands into grief-stricken claws (see *Figure 1-2*).

Step 4: Commence anguished raving. (Note: Since the purpose of this warm-up is to prepare you for the untimely or catastrophic death of a colleague or lover, you may also cry out the name of the deceased or possibly an imprecation against any or all of the following: a supreme being, death itself, or the generally unjust and chintzy nature of the universe. Also acceptable are cries of "Noooo!!!" or "Why!?!?")

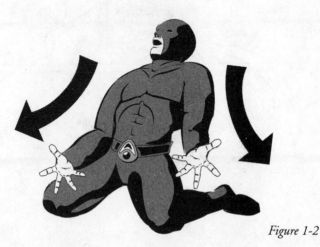

Figure 1-2

Ill-tempered Dragon Pose

Step 1: Stand with your feet shoulder-width apart. Your hands should hang loosely (but not limply) by your sides.

Step 2: Slide your right foot forward, keeping your pelvis balanced between your feet, until you're forced to flex each knee slightly.

Step 3: While raising your chin, lift your right arm straight ahead of you until it forms a 110-degree angle to your torso. Spread your fingers slightly and angle your hand as if reaching out toward something (see *Figure 1-3*). (Note: To receive the full benefit of this exercise, imag-

Figure 1-3

ine yourself threatening, warning, confronting, or like-wise addressing a supervillain or other miserable cur. You may also pretend to be witnessing a scene of unimaginable horror, a scene that you are, despite your many abilities, utterly powerless to stop.)

WHAT TYPE ARE YOU?

Before we move on to the specific honing exercises, let's take a moment to discuss the nine power classes and also introduce you to the Bureau of Meta-Human Affairs' hero classification system. While you have no doubt heard superheroes referred to as "knights," "avengers," or even "paladins," you may not have been aware of the fact that these terms are more than simple expressions of adulation; they also serve an organizational function. This is not a ranking system—for example, a "paladin" is not necessarily a better superhero than a "knight"—but simply a handy way for researchers and scholars to distinguish between heroes with more than one superpower.* In fact, you shouldn't feel obligated to tell anyone your type if you don't want to—remember, your actions make you a hero, not your powers.

How to Find Your Heroic Type

First, find your superpower(s) using the nine power classes outlined on the next page.

---

*Author's Note: That said, I know that many young or inexperienced heroes tend to fixate on their type, and some even try to acquire an extra superpower in order to "move up" in the rankings. While I never like to discourage anyone interested in self-improvement, there is a point at which injecting yourself with untested pharmaceutical substances or bathing in toxic sewage becomes obsessive and creepy instead of admirable.

SUPERPOWER QUICK REFERENCE CHART		
	Superpower	Symptoms May Include
	Flight	Flying, levitating, persistent floating
	Super-Strength	Excessive brawniness, often accompanied by intense periods of mightiness
	Invulnerability	Imperviosity and a general sense of well-being
	Psionic	Telepathy, telekinesis, possible baldness
	Magus	Standoffishness, pointy ears, unwarranted addition of letter "k" to end of word "magic"
	Super-Speed	Zipping, zooming, some headlong dashing
	Transmutation	Pervasive physiological enhancement, often accompanied by shape-shifting (Note: absence of human features does not necessarily indicate loss of humanity)
	Energy Projection/ Manipulation	Sometimes painful emission of beams or rays, also: godlike ability to control weather, magnetic fields, etc.
	Crimefighter	Exo-battlesuit, quaint weapons, unquenchable thirst for vengeance

Now, using the quick reference chart, determine whether you are a:

- **Knight** (0–1 superpower)
- **Champion** (2 superpowers)
- **Crusader** (3 superpowers)
- **Avenger** (4 superpowers)
- **Paladin** (5+ superpowers)

THE NEW PROMETHEANS: 1908–1934

"Though some researchers have argued that meta-humans existed in this country as early as the 1860s, it wasn't until the beginning of the twentieth century that they first appeared in the form in which we have come to know them: as *superheroes*. Though today we have eight different formal power classes, in the early 1900s, when heroes such as the Crimson Comet (who could fly for brief periods of time, thanks to his 'mathematical solution to the problem of *air thickness!*') and the Phantom Dynamo (a scientist whose 'Vitamin Z-59' provided him with incredible strength) were active, the scientific community would only recognize three—Flight, Super-Speed, and Invulnerability. Furthermore, throughout the 1920s, these same scientists continued to insist that the manifestation of these powers was due to a medical condition known as 'Drake's dropsy' or, more commonly, 'bewildered liver.'

"Nonetheless, the New Prometheans, as these heroes were known, captivated a world already swept away by the giddy excesses of the Jazz Age. Known as 'fly-boys' and 'super-sixes,' they inspired hit songs such as 'Moochie the Mask' and dances such as 'The Super-Streak.' Ultimately, even the scientific establishment was forced to accept the fact that superpowers could not be explained away as symptoms of an obscure illness. The revolutionary work of open-minded young scientists such as R. H. K. Bautz and Leland Kevin Maher forced the scientific establishment to embrace not only new elements such as vibranium, impervium, and Element X, but also other things that we now take for granted, such as gravitron particles and antaenic cells."   —from *A Decade in the Clouds: America and the Rise of the New Prometheans,* by Roland Foster

Chapter One

Flight

Though millions of people dream of flying, these are often subconscious expressions of sexual desire that have little in common with the experience of flight as a superpower. Far from being the stuff of erotic reverie, flight is, in fact, one of the most demanding of all the power classes, and it's not unusual for Flight Class heroes (FCHs) to spend several years simply developing the skills and techniques needed in order to master the unfamiliar medium of their atmospheric arena.

MIGHTY STRENGTHS AND TRAGIC FLAWS OF THE FCH	
Mighty Strengths	**Tragic Flaws**
Often possesses heightened reflexes and uncanny agility	Heightened reflexes and uncanny agility match up poorly against heat-seeking missiles and psionic force bolts
May attain cruising altitudes of up to 12,000 meters, with an average speed of about 5,000 km/hour	Prolonged exposure to such altitudes frequently results in excessive doses of harmful UV

(though some FCHs are capable of achieving faster-than-light speeds)	rays, chapped skin, and red, irritated eyes; your actual speed may vary
Confers the strategic and tactical advantages of the "high ground," thus allowing surveillance and close-air support	Also confers the strategic and tactical disadvantage of becoming an immediate "target" for all supervillains with ranged weapons
Offers enhanced mobility and permits hero to attack from a variety of unexpected directions	This advantage is neutralized by physically constrained and/or non-air environments (e.g., Mole-City, Dark Atlantis, root cellars, etc.)

FCH HONING EXERCISES

Basic Launch Exercise

This basic Flight Class pose (also sometimes referred to as *Aimless Lotus*) is the key to mastering both the launch and landing phases of superpowered flight. Make sure that you have plenty of room before beginning the exercise. Also, until you get more comfortable combining the different poses, I recommend that you perform this exercise out of doors, where you won't have to worry about smashing through a roof or skylight.

Step 1: Stand with your feet about shoulder-width apart. Your arms should be at your sides, palms facing inward. Relax your hips and allow your pelvis to open—remember, tight, restricted hips will block the subtle flow of energy

that's essential to maintaining proper superpower con-
ductivity.

Step 2: Slowly exhale while raising your arms up over your head
(see *Figure 1-4*). As you do so, carefully open and rotate
your hands until your palms are facing outward.

Figure 1-4

Step 3: Maintain this pose while continuing to breathe deeply and honestly. At the same time, do one of the following:

- Extend your wings until they have achieved their fullest expression; angle your wingtips forward slightly and confirm that your primary flight feathers are not molting or on fire.
- Instinctively activate the mysterious complex of nodes in your brain that enable you to manipulate your body's gravitron particles.

Step 4: Let your shoulders drop back slightly while you raise and lift your head. As soon as you confirm that the way is clear, allow yourself to slowly break free from gravity's harsh embrace. As your feet leave the ground, keep breathing and focus on keeping your spine as straight as possible to help stabilize your ascent.

Step 5: Repeat for prescribed number of reps. To land, simply reverse the order of the positions, remembering to flex your knees slightly upon touchdown.

Excelion Maneuver, Third Variation

As you become more confident in your flying technique, you may want to begin attempting more difficult maneuvers. While I cover one of the most popular ones here, you should also check out *Captain Airship's Big Book of Flying Techniques You Never Thought You Could Do* if you want to broaden your repertoire of in-flight tactics.

The following technique operates on a little-known principle of space-time dynamics that, essentially, establishes a direct relationship between the flow of time and the earth's rotation, thereby enabling you to reverse or accelerate time by manipulating the direction of and rate at which the planet turns on its axis.* Why would this be useful? Well, just think of all the times you've been late to work, or said something you shouldn't have, or watched millions die because you were too slow to save them, and thought to yourself: "If only I had the power to turn back time, then maybe I could put things right."

Step 1: Navigate out to the edge of the atmosphere, also known as "the part just before space." From here, the curve of the earth should become apparent, and beyond it, the cosmos. Don't be surprised if you quickly being to lose feeling in your fingers and toes. The temperature at this altitude is usually around minus 124 degrees Celsius. Wear a warm hat.

Step 2: Begin flying as fast as you can. If you want to reverse time, be sure to fly *against* the earth's rotation. On the other hand, if you want to accelerate time, fly *with* the earth's rotation. It is vitally important that you not confuse these two. For example, if you are trying to reverse time in order to defuse a radiomutation bomb planted by *Dr. Shellfish,* and instead you accidentally accelerate time, you will in fact be *helping* him carry out his diabolical plot. And let me tell you, you do not want to become known as the guy who "accelerated time and

---

*Editor's Note: This is an advanced technique, and should only be attempted with the assistance of an experienced and fully licensed Flight Class mentor.

helped turn everyone into giant, sociopathic oysters."
I've been through that hell, and man, it is not pretty.

Step 3: Each forced rotation of the earth forward or backward is
roughly equivalent to sixty of our Earth seconds. Therefore, if you want to reset events three minutes into the
past, you would fly contrary to the earth's natural rotation until you had halted and then reversed its momentum, and then count off three rotations before reversing
it once again and returning it to its natural course. Always err on the side of caution: if you think you might
need to go back three minutes and forty-two seconds
into the past, because that's the exact moment when the
earthquake destroyed Hoover Dam, don't try to measure
off forty-two sixtieths of a rotation. Instead, play it safe
and reverse time for a full four rotations.

Step 4: This is not only the most important step in manipulating time, it's also the one most people seem to forget.
After you've finished accelerating or reversing the tem-
poral flow, it's very important that you remember to return the planet to its normal rotation. I really can't stress
enough how important this is. You'd be surprised at how
often even experienced heroes will reverse time and then
forget to get it moving in the right direction again.

Chapter Two

Super-Strength

As a hero whose powers fall along the Super-Strength Class spectrum, you can look forward to someday becoming part of that select group of heroes known for doggedly grappling with titanic supervillains, cheerfully punching their way through steel bunkers, and avidly bludgeoning recalcitrant archenemies with the business end of some form of public transportation (for example, buses, trains, light rail, and so forth—you may be interested to learn that it's official policy for public sector vehicles to be pre-tested for secondary use as meta-human weapons).

HELPFUL HINT ALERT!
The following are the posted Bureau of Meta-Human Affairs (BMHA) requirements that must be met in order to qualify for recognition as a Super-Strength Class Hero.

- "Clean and jerk" an aircraft carrier
- Bench-press the Spratly Islands (or its equivalent) at least a dozen times

- Create a measurable seismic disturbance (plus 3 or greater on the Richter scale) by pounding your fists or stomping your foot against the earth
- Rip a metro-area phone book in half
- Execute a standing broad-jump that covers at least five kilometers
- Curl a Volkswagen Passat (three sets of ten reps)
- Hurl a fully loaded cement mixer a minimum of eight hundred meters
- Perform at least ten pull-ups (pull-ups must be performed using manly overhand grip)

MIGHTY STRENGTHS AND TRAGIC FLAWS OF THE SSCH

Mighty Strengths	Tragic Flaws
Enables hero to perform great feats of sturdiness, including bending steel girders with bare hands, juggling forklifts, and manfully hefting boothfuls of Cracker Barrel patrons	Less immobile or inanimate adversaries may insist on complicating such stirring displays of brute force by taking evasive action or simply whomping you with a high-powered laser from fifty meters out
Liberates one from the day-to-day impediments faced by the merely well-muscled, who are forced to rely on bulky or inconvenient levers, fulcrums, or Mexican day-laborers	Will likely become addicted to painkillers prescribed to treat chronic lower-back pain; may wind up as eccentric, Percoset-addicted shut-in who wanders

in order to accomplish most feats of strength	naked through secret headquarters compulsively munching on bouillon cubes
Gives one the power to stop runaway freight trains, turn aside the waters of a mighty flood, and catch planet-smashing meteors using a giant, specially made meteor-catching mitt	People may get lazy and start expecting you to also find the remote control, make their beds, help sort their recycling, and do something about that smell

SSCH HONING EXERCISE

Impudent Willow Pose
In this exercise we're going to focus on developing your ability to lift and hurl objects with high destructive potential, specifically: a bus. Be sure to ask a partner to spot you before attempting this maneuver.

Step 1: Select a bus to lift and hurl. (Note: Not all buses are approved for superheroic use, so be sure to check before lifting and hurling any bus or similar public transportation device. If you're not sure or can't seem to find the label, you can go to the BMHA Web site and check the model number against their master list.)

Step 2: Assume a hip-wide position. Your knees should be slightly bent. Flexing your knees deeply, crouch down and grasp the bottom rim of the bus. Be sure to get a grip on the vehicle's frame, and not just the shell, otherwise you're likely to end up simply ripping off a useless fragment of the bus (which will not even be worth hurling).

Step 3: Flex your knees until your hips descend to about the level of your hands. Make your back as flat as possible. Inhale deeply.

Step 4: Slowly begin to pull the bus away from the ground by extending your knees. Exhale slowly throughout this movement. Be careful not to jerk the bus—focus on lifting it instead.

Step 5: Once the bus passes your knees, rocket it toward your chest and up over your head by yanking your shoulders toward your ears and thrusting upward with your hips.

Step 6: At the bus rises above your head, use its momentum to toss it up in the air slightly and readjust your grip (see

Figure 1-5

Figure 1-5). You are now ready to hurl the bus at a robotic dinosaur or cosmic space beast (see *Figure 1-6*).

Figure 1-6

DID YOU KNOW . . .

. . . that some Super-Strength heroes get their power from "geo-force vibrations"? Geo-force vibrations, of course, are the sub-planetary energy waves that sustain all living things. Interestingly, ancient mystics intuited the existence of geo-force vibrations, or GFVs, as long ago as 300 BC, referring to them as, variously, "the song of Gaia," "the fecund trembling of the earth-womb," or something that translates as either "the harmonious voice of the stone-spirits" or "bad yams go bagpipe double-ply."

Chapter Three

Invulnerability

Though the Invulnerability Class superpowers may lack some of the appeal of the newer classes, for my money there's no better meta-ability you can have, particularly when combined with another superpower such as Flight or Super-Strength. Invulnerability is the ultimate complementary superpower, enhancing the effectiveness of other power classes by enabling you to, for instance, punch through a steel wall without shattering half the bones in your body, or fly at Mach speeds without being scorched by atmospheric friction.

MIGHTY STRENGTHS AND TRAGIC FLAWS OF THE ICH	
Mighty Strengths	**Tragic Flaws**
Virtually guarantees a happy-go-lucky existence free from the workaday worries caused by unsightly bullet wounds, painful acid scars, festering laser burns, meteorite bruising, plutonium rash, strontium lesions, uranium itch,	Despite much-touted immunity to sticks, stones, atomic weapons, etc., names may still prove unexpectedly painful

spankings, sloth maulings, frostbite, hickory welts, etc.	
Renders one shatterproof, weather-proof, friction-proof, leakproof, bulletproof, childproof, bombproof, rustproof, puncture-proof, and stain-resistant	Unfortunately, you will have one small, fairly life-threatening sensitivity to an exotic type of radiation or rare alien mineral; even worse, pretty much everyone will know all about it, including: what it is, where to get it, and the optimal method of administering it

DID YOU KNOW...

...that Invulnerability Class powers are often the result of unsually high levels of absorbinium cells? As you may already be aware, absorbinium cells are the mysteriously elastic cells that help cushion our body's joints. They're also the reason that our knees don't shatter when we skip rope or go after a jump ball. Most people have between 3.5 and 3.8 million absorbinium cells per cubic millimeter of their body (3.1 million is considered to be the bare minimum necessary to absorb the impacts of daily life). However, that's a far cry from the IC hero, whose absorbinium levels are often *12 to 15,000 times greater* than those found in average humans!

IC HONING EXERCISE

Obviously, since Invulnerability is a passive superpower, it's not practical to attempt to develop or hone it further. What we can work on, however, is overcoming your now-pointless self-preservative aversion to things like fire, electrocution, high-powered rifles, lead pencils, solar flares, rusty nails, and meteorite impacts. These quaint vestiges of your former vulnerability and mortality no longer serve any useful purpose and at this point only confound your attempts to realize the full extent of your potential.

The Immelman Release

For the following exercise, you will need a toaster, a large waterproof container, and a steady flow of electricity.

Step 1: Fill a bathtub or other container (one large enough to hold you as well as ten gallons of liquid) with warm water. Lower yourself into it or at least put your feet in.

Step 2: Grasp the toaster between your hands and hold it in front of you at about waist-height (see *Figure 1-7*). Next, release toaster, making sure that it falls into the water. (Note: Toaster should be plugged into nearby electrical outlet—if you do not plug in the toaster you won't enjoy the full benefits of this exercise.)

Step 3: Unplug toaster and replace any blown fuses. You may notice a slight tingling sensation. See your physician if this persists for more than a few hours.

Step 4: Repeat this exercise daily. If it starts to feel too easy, you may substitute a three-hundred-meter freefall, game of Russian roulette, or forward roll through a wood chipper.

Figure 1-7

DID YOU KNOW . . .

. . . that today the study of Invulnerability Class powers is almost
an afterthought among meta-human scholars and researchers?
It's true: generous government research grants, the promise of
tenure, and the constant pressure to publish in peer-reviewed
journals such as the *New England Journal of Super-Physiology*
have driven today's brightest scientists to focus primarily on
areas such as organic energy morphification and omni-beam
transduction. In these fields of study, even a small breakthrough
can result in television appearances, book deals, and one's own
top-secret research facility. Most of what we know about Invul-

nerability comes from the journals of the famed scientist-hero *Professor Infinity.* These journals, discovered in 1994 following Infinity's disappearance during the *Phantom Wars,* contain what even today is regarded as the most comprehensive body of work in this area. For example:

"Concerning Subject X . . . Found to be impervious even to extremely harmful or lethal physical stimuli, including . . . extremes of temperature, deadly projectiles (rocks, bullets, buses, etc.), crushing weights, global warming, paper cuts, mayonnaise, SUV rollovers, Communism, horseradish . . . [Although] apparently indestructible, further research . . . has revealed that some IT meta-humans are in fact susceptible to a specific type of attack or weapon, for example, exposure to a particular kind of radiation or to some fragment of their POO."*

---

*Planet of Origin

Chapter Four

Psionic

Even as the fortunes of other power classes rise and fall, the demand for experienced Psionic Class heroes (PCHs) has remained steady, particularly among heroic organizations, where the unique abilities of the PCH provide a valuable complement to Super-Strength or Energy Projection types. This is good news for you, the prospective PCH, since it's a strong indication that your budding powers, which may include telepathy, telekinesis, and astral projection, will guarantee you some extra degree of job security throughout your career.

| MIGHTY STRENGTHS AND TRAGIC FLAWS OF THE PCH ||
Mighty Strengths	Tragic Flaws
Grants the uncanny ability to reach out with one's mind to probe, fondle, and even manipulate the thoughts of others	Are helpless against androids, cyborgs, and stubbornly genocidal supercomputers; also: pistols, letter-openers, zombie hordes, supermodels, mad cows, and Scientologists

May manifest as the awesome capacity to do things—like add fabric softener or snuff out an entire planet—using only one's mind; other telekinetic abilities may include psychically lifting and hurling objects, altering a material's molecular structure, and bending spoons	Excessive telekinetic activity can result in temporary or even permanent mental strain or damage; symptoms may vary, from forgetting how to use your socks to filing a restraining order against adverbs
Enables one to break free from the confines of the earthly body and sally forth in astral form to mix it up with similarly disembodied foes	May all just be a bunch of New Age crap

PCH HONING EXERCISE

Uncanny Tortoise Pose

Step 1: Begin by relaxing your neck and shoulders. Your arms should be by your sides. Since this exercise will be accomplished solely through the power of thought, you may perform it either seated in a lotus position or standing in the pose known as *Aroused Cricket*.

Step 2: Focus on your breath. Every inhalation should be a conscious act of healing and cleansing. Inhale, count to ten, and then exhale slowly. Remember, for breathing to be successful, one must do it constantly (i.e., several times a minute for the rest of your life).

Step 3: Keeping your elbows locked, raise your arms out and up until they form an unbroken line with your shoulders. Now, bending your arms at the elbow, bring your hands toward your head.

Step 4: As your hands approach your head, extend the index finger and thumb of each hand so that your fingers come to rest on your temples (see *Figure 1-8*). (Note: Psionic-types are often hilariously uncoordinated. Be careful not to poke yourself in the eye.)

Step 5: Flex your brain or your cerebral cortex or whatever and start to use your psionic powers. Depending on the type of power you have, you may be able to read people's minds; exert a form of mind-control over defenseless

Figure 1-8

brains; start fires; or physically manipulate objects (as
seen in *Figure 1-9,* where a Psi-type hero is opening a
garage door from nearly one hundred feet away!).

Figure 1-9

Chapter Five

Magus

Though you'll find that many of the superpowers exercised by the Magus Class hero (MCH) seem identical to those wielded by members of the other power classes—for example, Flight, Super-Strength, and even Transmutation—the crucial distinction lies in the source of the MCH's powers. Unlike other superheroes, whose abilities are the result of their alien physiology, unnatural origin, or accelerated mutagenics, MCHs are not even technically meta-humans. In most cases, their powers are derived from enchanted objects, mystical bloodlines, or simple incantations that tap into the powerful magickal energies that bind and animate our universe.

MIGHTY STRENGTHS AND TRAGIC FLAWS OF THE MCH	
Mighty Strengths	**Tragic Flaws**
Enables one to walk untouched through the howling Otherworlds, unlock the arcane secrets of the Eye of Kra-Shyra, and thoroughly	After a while, you may start to come across as either miserably pretentious or some kind of "Goth fag"

tamper with forces beyond your control	
Gives one the power to act as a mystic guardian, standing alone against the demon hordes of the Shadowlands that seek to breach the dimensional gates and ravage our unsuspecting world	There tends to be a lot of down time between mystic breaches
Allows one to wield powerful magicks through the casting of spells, uttering of incantations, or gentle stroking of mystical objects	May end up spending a lot of time presiding over animal sacrifices, shopping around for newt gizzards, and just generally reeking of cheap incense

MCH HONING EXERCISE

Secret Mystic Fighting Pose #27

For this exercise you will need a pair of dumbbells, the Orb of Mammaru, and a training partner.

Step 1: Begin by standing with your feet shoulder-width apart. (Note: If you find it more comfortable, you may also sit or hover eerily using a Floskarian Disc of Levitation.)

Step 2: With your partner standing no more than five feet away, grasp the dumbbells in either hand and hold them in front of your thighs or at your side, palms facing in. Inhale slowly.

Step 3: While remaining mindful of your form, raise the dumb-bells. Be careful not use your shoulders, and pause just before full flexion of your biceps.

Step 4: As you exhale, surprise your partner by mystically extracting his soul and imprisoning it in the Orb of Mammaru (see *Figure 1-10*).

Figure 1-10

DID YOU KNOW...
... that while the term "superhero" is very much the product of our modern, industrial society, the idea of the superhero is found in every age and culture known to man? In fact, the very first "superheroes" were the shamans, druids, and wizards of the Earth's ancient civilizations. Centuries later, as archaeologists and adventurers stumbled upon the powerful secrets of mankind's

earliest guardians, they vowed to continue their predecessors'
never-ending battle against the forces of evil.

Not surprisingly, these young men and women, finding inspiration in their occult heritage as well as in the culture around
them, chose to fight crime disguised, variously, as mythical beings
(see the *Red Djinn*), the reincarnation of ancient god-kings or
warrior-shamans (see the *Mighty Zal-Mak*), or even vaudeville
magicians (see *Mr. Mystery*), complete with tuxedo and sometimes
even a turban. The range of powers and abilities these supernatural warriors exhibited in their early battles against injustice (powers that remain much the same for today's MCHs) included:

- Invoking and harnessing the power of supernatural creatures
- Weaving magicks of varying intensity and almost limitless effect
- Summoning demons from the Middle Realms
- Communicating with the dead
- Opening portals into the five dimensions of the Arcana as
  well as the sixteen (now twenty-four) known magickal realms
- Activating and wielding enchanted weapons and tools (e.g.,
  rings, amulets, mysterious orbs)

In addition, many of these early MCHs discovered that the
habitual use of their arcane powers triggered the development of
other talents, such as the ability to fly, to perform great feats of
strength, and even to survive, unscathed, tremendous impacts or
explosions.

Chapter Six

Super-Speed

In the one-hundred-yard dash against evil, the Super-Speed Class hero (SPCH) always comes in first. Despite being unfairly discriminated against and often relegated to a support role due to the "narrowly specialized" or "one-dimensional" nature of their superpowers, SPCHs have made an inspiring comeback recently by learning to be more creative in the deployment of their meta-abilities. No longer content to simply dodge laser beams, catch bullets, dizzy criminals to the point of unconsciousness, or kick up a whirlwind by running in super-fast circles, Super-Speed types have found new relevance through attacks such as Maneuver 14, otherwise known as the "400-punches-in-under-a-second attack," and Variation 9 (that is, using one's super-speed to actually travel back in time or "phase" into other dimensions).*

---

*Use extreme caution when attempting any of these maneuvers on artificial turf.

MIGHTY STRENGTHS AND TRAGIC FLAWS OF THE SPCH	
Mighty Strengths	**Tragic Flaws**
Endows one with unimaginable swiftness and super-fast reflexes, thus permitting heroic as well as everyday actions to be performed at nearly the speed of light	Try thinking about baseball
Enables one to accelerate to temporal and/or interdimensional escape velocities and travel to other dimensions, back into the past, through time and space, etc.	Ancient civilizations are insufferably quaint, while futuristic societies of super-intelligent apes regard you as a hairless novelty; also, you may end up unwittingly having sex with ancestors, descendents
Facilitates such rapid molecular vibration that one can actually "phase" through solid objects	You may experience a slight burning sensation

SPCH HONING EXERCISE

Princeton Repetitions
While not absolutely essential, it's a good idea to use a training partner for this exercise.

Step 1: Find an open space, such as a park or an athletic field. Start with a light jog at first, then gradually increase your speed until you're approaching escape velocity.

Figure 1-11

Step 2: After you break the sound barrier and the objects around you appear to be growing elongated or distorted as you pass them, begin running in a circular pattern (see *Figure 1-11*). You may choose to run in either a clockwise or counterclockwise direction, as long as you're consistent.

Step 3: Soon you should start to notice "a violently rotating column of air" forming at the center of your circle. This is what is known as a tornado (also sometimes called a cyclone or "death-funnel"). Tornados such as the one you've just created are capable of winds in excess of three hundred miles per hour and can carve a spectacular swath of destruction through trailer parks and giant berserker robots alike.

Step 4: Having successfully created this unstoppable force of nature, now is a good time to ask your partner to place an anonymous call to the National Weather Service and then immediately head for shelter.

THE FORGOTTEN SUPERPOWER

"The Super-Speed Class Hero, or SPCH, though technically the most recent heroic classification to be recognized by the Bureau of Meta-Human Affairs, is often categorized with the other New Promethean powers—i.e., Flight, Super-Strength, Invulnerability, and Magus—for the purposes of research and also as a gesture of respect for an oft-overlooked power type. The fact is that although the daring exploits of SPCHs such as *Lickety-Lad* and the *Masked Meteor* compare favorably with those of other renowned New Promethean heroes, SPCHs were widely held to be nothing more than defective FCHs (Flight Class Heroes). The scientists of the time, whose instruments were unable to detect either the *quick spectrum* or these heroes' delicate *propelloplasm cells*, simply assumed that Super-Speed was an inferior variation of the FCHs' own gravitron manipulation process.

"Thus, before 1968, all scientific inquiry into the nature of Super-Speed powers focused on what was 'wrong' with the SPCH. Scientists hoping to make a name for themselves by 'curing' the SPCH of this 'unmanly atmospheric phobia' subjected these heroes to all manner of treatment—from electro-shock therapy to temporarily sealing them inside 'recuperative cocoons' of Vulcanized rubber—in the hope of restoring their 'native affinity for the vault of heaven . . . and the distant horizon.'

"Such attitudes remained fundamentally intact until the late '60s, when a young scientist named Winston Shephard Boucher joined the staff of New York University's prestigious Stonecroft research facility and resolved to make the SPCH the focus of his work there. Though Boucher's contemporaries dismissed his findings, his groundbreaking research found a ready audience in a new generation of meta-human scholars and young, alienated superheroes seeking to change the status quo. United by their idealism and sustained by the strength of Boucher's conclusions, these determined upstarts demanded a wholesale reevaluation, not only of the SPCH and his unique talents and achievements, but also of what it meant to be a superhero. While the effects of this 'capeless revolution'—the cape of course being seen as the symbol of a repressive superheroic patriarchy—extended far beyond the SPCH, they are too subtle and numerous to be thoroughly recounted here." —from *Living at Escape Velocity: A History of Super-Speed,* by Niles Jugland

Chapter Seven

Transmutation

I f you're wondering about whether you might be eligible for recognition as a Transmutation Class hero (TCH), then the first thing you need to do is consider your secret origin. Unlike other power classes (with the possible exception of the Magus Class), TCHs are classified according to the source of their powers. So ask yourself: Was I bathed in omega radiation during a secret weapons test? Or bombarded by cosmic rays during an aborted interstellar expedition? Has my body begun spontaneously evolving at the cellular level?

WARNING

As virtually all Transmutation Class heroes will express powers that fall into other classifications, at this time the BMHA has released only provisional guidelines for Transmutation Class recognition. Continue to check with your local branch for release of the formal qualifications for TCH recognition. The following meta-human characteristics are the work of the author, and in no way represent the formal declaration of guidelines by the Bureau of Meta-Human Affairs.*

---

*This notice provided in accordance with Section 1.d. of the BMHA Classification Protocol.

Mutation is unpredictable, and results in superpowers that are, in all practical senses of the word, limitless. Though TCHs may share important similarities with other recognized power classes, their powers are often unique and unprecedented. However, for the purposes of our discussion here, I've divided them into two groups: *simple transformation* and *complex transformation.*

Simple Transformation

For many TCHs, genetic mutation results in a permanent state of superhuman enhancement, while for others it can mean the ability to execute a simplified physical transformation from one state to another (i.e., human to superhuman). While in either state (technically, Transmutation-types are the only superheroes that can truly be called "superhuman"), their powers may include aspects of some or all of the following:

- Super-Strength
- Invulnerability
- Flight
- Psi-powers
- Super-Speed
- Energy Projection/Manipulation (see next chapter)

However, these powers do not come about through mechanisms such as gravity manipulation or the activity of absorbinium molecules, but are purely the result of radical cellular mutation. Subsets of this group include *simple enhancement* and *complex enhancement.*

Also, some Transmutation Class heroes may experience transformation-related side effects or a range of unpredictable but complementary powers, such as:

- Excessive size
- Outlandish musculature
- Superfluous nipples
- Altered mental state
- Atypical pigmentation (e.g., green skin, blue hair, sunflower yellow eyes)
- The appearance of scales, fur, feathers, odd hairstyles, or blubber
- Advanced healing factor
- Doppler radar
- Adhesive extremities
- Heightened senses
- Horns

HELPFUL HINT ALERT!
While we all know that evil can strike at any time, what you may not have realized is that it often strikes at only the most inconvenient times: specifically, when you're out of costume and posing as a mild-mannered mortal. I can't tell you how many times I've been at a dinner party or gallery opening only to be called away to battle a smog-monster or some such. What is the proper etiquette in these situations? And how do you excuse yourself without offending your date or host?

- Begin by thanking everyone for a lovely evening. Also, if you feel comfortable doing so, demonstrate your sincerity by composing and performing a brief sonnet or performance piece. (Note: This would not be appropriate if you're simply leaving a business meeting or ducking out of class.)
- Next, offer a short but gracious apology. You may also want to come up with an excuse to explain your hasty departure and forestall any suspicion as to your true identity. Acceptable excuses include, "I have cancer," and "My water just broke."
- Minimize any awkwardness by promising to call the next day and make lunch plans. Leave immediately; don't linger. Once you're out of sight, duck into an empty supply closet or vacant phone booth and change into your costume.

Complex Transformation

Similar to the *simple transformation* discussed earlier, *complex transformation* also involves a shift from a human state to a superhuman state, but in this case the transformation is much more radical, usually involving a transition from a human physiology to an inhuman or even nonorganic constitution. In addition to the range of powers exhibited in the *simple* state, *complex* transformations also sometimes involve devastating *energy* or *matter manipulation* powers (note: you may not always have complete control over these powers). Transmutation Class heroes who exhibit *complex* characteristics can often be identified by their nonhuman appearance, as they may appear to be composed entirely of some other element, such as:

- Fire
- Ice
- Brightly colored rock
- Electricity
- Organic steel
- Sand
- Water
- Obsidian
- Magma
- Elastinium
- Chocolate pudding
- Cosmic energy

MIGHTY STRENGTHS AND TRAGIC FLAWS OF THE TCH	
Mighty Strengths	**Tragic Flaws**
Radical cellular mutation manifests in a series of profound molecular transformations, ultimately unlocking a fantastic variety of powers, such as the ability to shoot colorful bolts of energy from one's eyes or morph into a being of living fire	There is also every chance that, due to the pointlessly cruel process of random genetic mutation, you'll be neither a powerful "human torch" nor a walking laser cannon, but some poor schlub with a testicle growing out of his armpit

TCH HONING EXERCISE

The Way of the Impudent Fist

To perform this exercise you will need a biker bar, truck stop, honky-tonk, or other disreputable nightspot. You will also need to dress in tight-fitting, inelastic, imperfectly-stitched clothing (this applies to everything except your pants, which should be made of a new miracle fabric that will stretch and maintain its shape even if your body should happen to increase to several times its usual size).

Step 1: Enter the workout area in your "normal" state. Sit down in the first vacant seat you can find. Remember to look as much like an asthmatic nebbish as possible.

Step 2: The seat you've chosen will invariably be the *exact same seat* favored by the ringleader of the local gang of rednecks/truckers/werewolf drug lords, etc. This honest mistake on your part will result in a confrontation of some kind, after which the ringleader and his gang will ridicule your manhood, beat you with pool cues, and then stuff you into a derelict refrigerator, abandoned mine shaft, or iron lung.

Step 3: You may become agitated. If this should happen, warn your tormentors that they must stop immediately or you may not be able to control yourself. (Note: Unfortunately, your warning will most likely be met with derision.)

Step 4: Unleash the awesome mutant power trapped in your cells. Wait until you're certain that A) your amazing transformation is complete, and B) you've shed most of your clothing.

Step 5: With a mighty roar and a series of sudden, violent movements, smash free of any confinements (see *Figure 1-12*). Since at this point you're very likely a twelve-foot-tall, two-ton, super-strong, nearly indestructible mutant juggernaut, your former tormentors are likely to either scuttle backward fearfully or be frozen in terror. Toss them around and generally bust up the place for at least twenty minutes, which is generally long enough for a good cardio workout. (Note: If this exercise begins to seem too easy, you can substitute a military base or alien homeworld for a truck stop or honky-tonk.)

Figure 1-12

DID YOU KNOW . . .

. . . that for years people believed that the goal of the Manhattan Project was to develop an atomic bomb? It's true! While today it's common knowledge that the Project was created to engineer new types of superheroes (with the Bomb being an unexpected and minor by-product of that effort), no one outside the innermost circles of power had a clue that three new power classes—Psionic, Transmutation, and Energy Projection/Manipulation—were actually the result of Manhattan Project experiments. That would probably still be the case today, had a series of top-secret documents—known collectively as the *Centurion Files*—not been leaked to Richard W. Lobel, at the time a relatively unknown investigative reporter toiling away at the city desk of the *New York Planet*. Lobel used the Centurion Files as the basis for his Pulitzer Prize–winning series *Inside the Los Alamos Mask Factory*.

Chapter Eight

Energy Projection and Manipulation

One of today's most exciting and relatively new superpower classifications is the Energy Projection/Manipulation Class (EPMC). EMPC powers have captured the imagination of the entire world. In fact, people everywhere are wandering unescorted around top-secret military installations and splashing themselves with unknown substances in hopes of being rewarded with EPMC powers.

Broadly characterized by their ability to act as a conduit for, or in some cases actually wield, various forms of energy, Energy Projection/Manipulation types often exhibit characteristics peculiar to other power classes as well. You should note that EPMC types are sometimes confused with Transmutation Class types, particularly ones who exhibit some limited mastery over fire or electricity. However, while TCHs must actually *become* a particular type of energy in order to control it (in a sense, merging with that energy), EPMCHs simply act as a conduit—their molecular structure is not altered by the experience. Some of the energies often wielded by EPMCHs include:

- Heat rays
- Repulsor beams
- Optic blasts
- "Dark energy" pulses
- Inviso-shields
- Plasma lances
- Concussion bolts
- Nova beams
- "Electro-darts"
- "Anti-aggression" fields

MIGHTY STRENGTHS AND TRAGIC FLAWS OF THE EPMCH	
Mighty Strengths	**Tragic Flaws**
Enables one to act as a living conduit or battery for powerful energies	Care should be taken whenever activating your power around water, as there's a significant risk that a catastrophic short-circuit could result; proper hygiene should be maintained through the vigorous applications of Wet-Naps to any soiled areas
Grants capacity to unleash the equivalent of 2,000 terrajoules (1.8 trillion BTUs) of energy in a single, devastating stream of tightly focused, evil-inhibiting power (in real terms, this is enough energy to kick the ass of a different super-	Recent studies have shown that excessive unleashing of such energies may result in side effects, including dry mouth, chronic grumpiness, and "floppy-bone" syndrome

villain every day for almost *two weeks*)	
Ability to wield and manipulate environmental energy, including magnetism, static electricity, and localized weather systems	Exercise caution when attempting to operate your powers while under the seductive influence of an evil mind-control device, dastardly mentalist, or slimy alien parasite that may be writhing around in your brainpan

EPMCH HONING EXERCISE

Position Prime, Subset C
To perform this exercise you will need a pair of dumbbells (a barbell is also acceptable).

Step 1: Place the weights in front of you. Stand with your feet about shoulder-width apart. Bend over and drop your buttocks so that your thighs are roughly parallel to the floor. Grasp the weights in an overhand grip, keeping your arms just outside of your calves and your chin up.

Step 2: Inhale deeply and honestly. Allow the cleansing intake of breath to chase away any self-doubt, spiritual blockages, or annoying commercial jingles.

Step 3: Exhale and slowly begin to straighten your body, pulling the weights up along the front of your legs.

Step 4: Reverse the movements as precisely as you can while keeping your knees open and your head up.

Step 5: Repeat for prescribed number of repetitions. If you start to feel a slight burning sensation in your lower back, immediately place the weights on the floor, step back, and reduce the offending exercise equipment to a heap of molten slag using your solar blasts (see *Figure 1-13*). (Note: If you do not have solar blasts, you may substitute optic blasts, heat vision, force beams, or any other sort of appropriately destructive radiation.)

Figure 1-13

Chapter Nine

Crimefighter Class (*Pending*)

Sometimes the greatest superpower of all is an insatiable hunger for justice, seasoned with just the slightest hint of vengeful wrath and served over a bed of warm bloodlust. So if you've been unsuccessful in your attempts to acquire superpowers, or simply feel a burning desire to immediately begin clearing the streets of villainous scum, you may want to consider becoming a Crimefighter Class Hero (CCH). It's not hard, provided you have good study habits, are self-motivated, and have recently witnessed the brutal murder of your family or loved ones.

Despite the fact that the BMHA has yet to formally recognize the CCH as an authentic power class, Crimefighters are a vital part of the superheroic community. Continue to check with your local BMHA branch for further information regarding the release of formal qualifications for CCH recognition.

MOST POPULAR CRIMEFIGHTER CLASS WEAPONS
Despite the advent of gunpowder and lasers, Crimefighter Class heroes have stubbornly persisted in using archaic or otherwise

hopelessly outdated weaponry. Here, for example, are some of the more popular and/or insane choices:

- Boomerangs
- Throwing knives
- Billy clubs
- Lariats
- Bow-and-arrows
- Gas pellets
- Bolos
- Small rocks
- The silent treatment
- Swords
- Their bare hands

MIGHTY STRENGTHS AND TRAGIC FLAWS OF THE CCH (*PENDING*)

Mighty Strengths	Tragic Flaws
Permits one, as a millionaire playboy industrialist, to legally plunder the organizational and financial resources of one's multinational conglomerate in order to create and maintain otherwise prohibitively expensive crimefighting vehicles and equipment	In the absence of any commercially viable product or service, your company will most likely spiral into an ugly bankruptcy; the storming of your corporate HQ by angry shareholders brandishing pitchforks is a likely event and should be planned for immediately
Cultivates a tough, unsentimental view of good and evil that permits	You'll probably be forced to listen to the eye-roll-inducing

the maiming or extermination of deserving criminals	"if-we-sink-to-their-level-we're-no-better-than-the-criminals" speech, not only from liberal politicians and misguided citizens, but even from fellow superheroes (who would secretly love to be the bad-ass mutha that you are but clearly lack the necessary testicular infrastructure)
Offers the chance to inspire others by decisively proving that true heroism is not about superpowers but about doing the right thing, fighting injustice in all its various forms, etc.	You would happily trade all that sanctimonious crap for the ability to fly

CCH HONING EXERCISE

O'Bannon Lifts

To perform this exercise you will need a pull-up bar and the help of a partner.

Step 1: Have your partner stand to either side of you. He or she should be about five feet away, or just out of arm's reach.

Step 2: Stretch your body upward and grasp the pull-up bar. Use an overhand grip. The distance between your hands should be slightly wider than your shoulders.

Step 3: With a fluid, explosive movement that begins in your spleen/bladder, pull yourself upward. Keep your head tilted up and your eyes focused on a spot about three feet beyond the pull-up bar itself.

Step 4: With your arms and shoulders deeply flexed, swing your hips and legs away from your partner. Hold this position

> **HELPFUL HINT ALERT!**
> If you're a hero whose weapon is a mystical sword that can slice through any substance known to man, or a set of unbreakable, razor-sharp claws that extend from the backs of your hands, then remember: even when seized by a berserker rage, don't muscle through the killing stroke, but instead let the blade(s) do the work.

tion briefly before unwinding your lower body and smashing your partner in the face (see *Figure 1-14*). (Note: If you're doing this exercise correctly you should see some blood or assorted viscera. If not, repeat exercise until you do.)

Figure 1-14

THE GREAT SCHISM

"All but a few scholarly monographs and obscure texts treat the *Valaxis Society* as nothing more than a merger between two complementary meta-human organizations. The fact is, however, that the push to create the Society sparked a bitterly divisive internal conflict, one that nearly destroyed the superheroic fraternity.

"Though the *Pallas Club*, which was formed in 1907, proclaimed itself to be 'the world's preeminent organization for the advancement of costumed gentlemen,' it was not the only such group in existence. In fact, in 1912, when the industrialist Ebeneezer Vanderfox and the famed superhero known as *Sixty-Minute Samson* were negotiating to buy the Fifth Avenue site of the Pallas Club's future Hall of Justice, the *Royal Institute of the Inexplicable* (initially conceived of as a magus-specific organ of the Royal Geographical Society) had already been in existence for nearly fifty years.

"An uneasy peace existed between the two groups until, in 1922, some of the members of the Institute, sensitive to the growing popularity of the superhero and recognizing (correctly) that this new age of rampant industrialization would benefit the scientifically generated hero far more than the wielder of strange magicks and enchanted helmets, attempted to not only join the Pallas Club, but also pressed for formal classification. While a small group of superheroes saw the benefits of unification and lobbied on behalf of the MCHs for recognition, the majority, spurred on by a fear of losing their 'native superhero identity,' fought back hard.

"Amid angry slogans such as 'There's nothing "super" about the supernatural!' and 'Just say no to the tuxedo!' disgruntled superheroes marched in the streets and, led by the idiosyncratic

Grey Gunslinger, even threatened to break away from the Pallas Club. Only the growing threat of an alliance between the *Council of Doom* and the *Phobos League* brought the various factions to the bargaining table, and even then, only after continued pressure from the American, British, Canadian, and French governments, was the Valaxis Society born." —from *The Great Gamble: The Uncertain Creation of the Valaxis Society,* by Frederick Hooper

Part Two

The Four Keys to a Successful Crime-fighting Career

Chapter Ten

Style, Substance, and Stain-resistance: Crafting the Perfect Alter Ego

We've all seen superheroes who have it (and you don't need X-ray vision or sonar-like enhancements to know what I'm talking about). We pass these heroes on the street and think to ourselves: "Perhaps it's something about the way they wear their cape, draped to one side with just a touch of authoritative playfulness. Or maybe it's the crisply tailored lines of their neutron-armor that seem to say, 'Look out, world, I'm here and I'm nigh-invulnerable!' Maybe it's even as simple as their accessories: a suggestive mask, that classic utility belt slung low across the hips, or those two darling lightning bolts mounted, *just so,* on their headgear."

So we study them, hoping to copy their seemingly effortless command of fashion, color, texture, and exotic weaponry. But somehow, we always fall short. We spend months shopping for that exact same cape, only to find that on us it looks about as sassy as a burlap sack. We blow our monthly costume allowance on a new exo-frame, but once we get it home, we realize that what it really says is, "Look out, world, I gained twenty pounds over the holidays!" And that timeless utility belt and those perky lightning bolts? Don't even ask.

LET'S MEET . . . BARON VON BLIMP, AKA THE INFLATABLE MAN!

Though even fans admit that Von Blimp is "probably not a member of any recognized aristocracy" and, in fact, "may not even be Prussian," this "elasticized airborne baddie" nevertheless "manages to infuse his criminal exploits with a certain grating foppishness." Offering a "welcome change of pace from the usual foaming-at-the-mouth types," Von Blimp uses his "miniature gas-synthesizing device" to generate the helium with which he "literally gorges his weirdly expandable self into weightlessness." Watch for him to "come bobbling malevolently toward you on a gentle night breeze," but "beware his deadly blimp-bombs and tendency to get entangled in high-tension wires."
—from *Mister Mental's Survey of Supervillains,* 2003 edition

(This evil-doer is just one of the many foes that have been carefully ranked and catalogued for you in the annual *Mister Mental's Survey of Supervillains.* Each year Mister Mental asks thousands of heroes what they think of the evil-doers they've battled over the past twelve months, and then uses their responses to summarize and rate each supervillain. While I've excerpted select listings from the survey under the "Let's Meet . . ." sidebar, I strongly recommend that you go out and pick up your own copy of Mister Mental's invaluable book.)

Deep down, we know we're just as stylish and accomplished as those other heroes, but for some reason, we can't seem to find a look that tells the world just how super we really are. So we make excuses: "It shrank when the *Electric Kaiser* nailed me with his heat ray," or "I think the saleswoman was actually the *Yellow Claw* in disguise, because there's no way this is a size 4!" We chase the latest styles: "I don't care if I am invulnerable, if the *Radioactive Ranger* is wearing a polylithoid helmet, then so am I!" We even resort to borrowing bits of other superheroes' names, costumes, or secret origin stories: "No, see, my costume has blue epaulets. The *Centurion*'s has red epaulets. They're totally different."

But no matter how carefully we copy their perfectly developed look, we still end up asking ourselves, "How come the same cape/mask/state-of-the-art battlesuit that worked so well for them makes me look like a hopelessly dowdy sidekick?" The answer to that question is simple. These heroes have something that can't be copied, something called:

A UNIQUE PERSONAL STYLE ALL THEIR OWN

In the last chapter we worked on honing your powers; now, I'm going to activate my super-stylist abilities and help you with your unique personal style. There are three components of any truly memorable unique personal style (or UPS): your **name,** your **secret origin story,** and your **costume.** Classic superheroes such as *Captain Stupendous* and *Miss Micro* knew this intuitively; their brilliant reinvention of such stale accessories as the cowl and the demi-cape have made it impossible to imagine them fighting crime in anything else. And who will ever forget the understated elegance of *Cinder-Block-Man*'s power gauntlets? Or the delicious chill you felt anytime you heard the name the *Vengeancer*? How about *Alpha-Girl* and her signature solar-goggles? Her vivid blend of tradition and technology made her an instant fashion icon, while her classic secret origin provided her with a welcome air of feminine sophistication.

But before I can help you create an authentic personal style, we need to figure out *who you really are.* And not just who you are, but also: How did you come by your special abilities? What sort of costume fits your crimefighting style? What kind of name reflects your crusading personality? Get ready, because in this chapter, we start to explore the wonderful, fascinating person known as *YOU*.

The smart hero knows how to look great without spending a bundle.

Step One: Choosing a Name

What is it about choosing a name that makes some superheroes just go to pieces? Interestingly enough, most of the problems I've encountered in this area are often due to a hero's inability to see him or herself as the rest of the world sees them. To help explain what I mean, I'd like to introduce you to someone. We'll call him Skipper.

When I first met Skipper, he'd just gotten back from the underworld, having been chosen to return to the mortal plane as the mystical incarnation of Justice. Now, the moment I met him, I knew that Skipper was going to make a great superhero. The problem was, Skipper didn't know that. And this was the root of his problem. Since Skipper couldn't see all the things that were so special about *Skipper,* he couldn't understand what others would see in him.

LET'S MEET . . . L.I.M.P.!

"Forget the agents of W.Y.R.M.—the evil organization of the future is L.I.M.P.!" Originally conceived of as "a nonprofit association providing health care and retirement planning services to the supervillain community," L.I.M.P. (the League of Irate Megalomaniacs and Para-humans) has since "gone global" and expanded the scope of its activities to include "all manner of diabolical enterprise." With a "colorful membership" that includes "alien overlords, sentient gorillas, evil mutants, unrepentant shoplifters, cloned dictators," and "certain reanimated pets," the agents of L.I.M.P. (led by their Supreme Leader) "are definitely behind" "some of the more interesting evil plots of the past few years," including "a muscle-canceling virus" and the "Medusa satellite."   —from *Mister Mental's Survey of Supervillains,* 2003 edition

Skipper's first obstacle was his name. But what is a name? As a superhero, your name is really just a reminder—to other heroes, supervillains, and the general public—of the qualities that make you the unique and special person that you are. In fact, the prejudicial effect of names like *Stupendous Man* or the *Vengeancer* has been well documented; during a recent double-blind, placebo-controlled study, researchers found that the mere mention of these superheroes caused even hardened evil-doers to experience a surge in adrenalin levels, a sudden drop in bladder content, and a heart rate that hovered somewhere between "panicky" and "organ donor."

But what if you're saying to yourself, "Okay, Doc, I got it. My name should reflect my heroic personality. It should inspire fear and loathing among the supervillain community. But how can I possibly come up with a name that does all that? I don't even know where to start!" Well, whether or not you realize it, you've *already* started! For example, did you know that many super-heroes have found the inspiration for their names in the events of their own origin stories (see the *Bog Devil, Captain Blunderbuss*)? Or in the type and nature of their superpowers (see *Projectile-Man, Doc Destiny*)? Maybe something memorable or unusual happened to you just prior to embarking on your superheroic ca-reer, something that almost seemed like an omen (perhaps you encountered an unusual animal or strange phenomenon)? This too could prove to be a rich source of inspiration.

Finally, don't overlook those aspects of *you* that make you a special and interesting person. Perhaps you've been so focused on your superpowers lately that you've forgotten about all your other hobbies and interests. For example, maybe you enjoy tinkering with ham radios. Or are involved in a local puppet troupe. Or love poking bloated roadside carcasses with a stick. Whatever it is, don't forget that these activities are often a treasure trove of ideas.

> "Some heroes are more memorable than others, not because they have vastly superior powers or are better crimefighters, but because they've created an unforgettable personal brand."   —All-American Amazon

The approaches I've outlined so far have yielded some very encouraging results in the past (in fact, after only a few sessions, one client of mine was able to recall a very inspiring encounter with a timber wolf that ultimately led him to adopt the now-famous name *Litterbox*). However, you may find that you need a little help getting started. In fact, so many of my clients were struggling to create appropriate names that I decided to develop the Superheroic Name Generator™ in order to help them.

To operate the Superheroic Name Generator™, simply select the most relevant options from columns A through E and apply them to the template. You may also opt to skip column B, and simply precede selections from column A with one of the

following: *Captain, Doctor, Professor, Saint,* or *Scoutmaster.* Use of
the article *the* is also acceptable. Note: Do not attempt to operate
the Superheroic Name Generator™ while evil or intoxicated.

SUPERHEROIC NAME GENERATOR™

_____ _____, _____ _____ of _____

     A   **B**   **C**   **D**   **E**

Column A	Column B	Column C	Column D	Column E
Blue	Man	Fearless	Defender	Truth
Crimson	Woman	Ripe	Crusader	Justice
Blond	Boy *or* Lad	Pro Bono	Warlord	Freedom
Masked	Girl, Gal, *or* Lass	Deliberate	Protector	Equality
Caped	Avenger	Careful	Consumer	Virtue
Magnifi-cent	Ghost	Cautious	Knight	Right-Thinking
Weightless	Beast	Reckless	Wrangler	Honesty
Daring	Phantom	Awe-Inspiring	Champion	Candor
Ice *or* Icy	Arrow	Cranky	Matador	Wisdom
Fire *or* Fiery	Lantern	Gritty	Cossack	Peace
Radioactive	Bread Machine	Supreme	Amazon	Booze

Wireless	Angel	Unsurpassed	Valkyrie	Germany
Electro-	Thing	Well-groomed	Berserker	All That Is Good
Dyna-	Torch	Chaste	Barbarian	Probity
Cosmic	Hound	Buoyant	Skirmisher	Literacy
Can-Do	Commando	Crisp	Conscript	Courteous Behavior
Flavorful	Scout	Keen	Advocate	Gentle-manly Conduct
Thrifty	Dervish	First-rate	Apologist	Civility
Fully Actualized	Titan	Top-drawer	Constable	Good Breeding
Invisible	Dental Hygienist	Unshrinking	Legal Guardian	The Privileged Few

Step Two: Crafting a Secret Origin Story

Despite the fact that 71 percent of citizens surveyed said that a hero's origin story would be "very or extremely interesting to me," this facet of the UPC remains an afterthought for many masked crusaders. This is too bad, because when you neglect your origin story, you forfeit one of the few tools you have to help you stand out in today's crowded superhero marketplace.

I recommend taking some time now, during the personal style development phase, to construct a clear and engaging

[Not sure this is the right tone... please see me]

▓▓▓▓▓▓▓▓▓

It all started because my so-called "manager," Brad — affectionately ~~referred~~ to around the ~~temp~~ pool as "Cocksucker" —

[where are you going with this?]

does not have even the slightest clue, and so when one of the antimatter venting chambers ~~started~~ giving off a hot reading, he totally freaked and made ME go down to check ~~it out~~. Like I'm cleared for Level 12! I mean, I'm just a ~~temp~~ And, I majored in English. Technically, I'm not even supposed to use the ~~office copy machine~~. But I go anyway, and as soon as the airlock opens, I get this feeling like I'm going to hurl, because everyone is totally dead! And I don't on Level 12 know why, exactly —something about the way the "super-agitated radiation interacted with my particular cell structure" — and let's all give ~~that~~ explanation a hearty round of shrug — but instead of killing me, the ~~stuff~~ gave me these nifty powers. So remember kids, that liberal arts degree isn't as worthless as your dad says!

[try "maverick scientist"]

["matter duplicator"]

[we?]

[GREAT DETAIL!!]

[Dead how? Burned, dissolved, etc? Be specific!]

[I'm confused...]

[specific!]

[Hmm...]

[Ending a little weak, but overall, nice first draft.]

[And watch the language, hero! DM]

narrative of how you acquired your new powers. Since I've found that most heroes tend to make the same mistakes when recounting the grisly or improbable events of their super-genesis, I've included here an early draft of one of my clients' origin stories, along with my comments. Please study it carefully, paying close attention to the areas I've highlighted.

Now, keeping in mind what you've learned, write your own origin story. Practice reading it aloud to a trusted friend or sidekick (only under rare circumstances should you practice in front of your archenemy or another supervillain). You also might find it helpful to videotape yourself, so that you can identify and eliminate distracting speaking habits, disconcerting facial ticks, and any other unsightly deformities.

Step Three: Shopping for a Costume

The right costume can flatter and flatten, lift and lengthen, intimidate, insinuate, and basically make us feel like, well, *superheroes*. But the wrong costume can do just the opposite. And unfortunately, too many of us are wearing things that frumpify, fatten, and flop. Take it from me: when you feel like you've got nothing to wear, you don't care who or what is trashing Summit City—you're not even leaving the house.

Why don't we just throw on a pair of tights, grab a cape from the hamper, and go deliver an ultimatum to that rampaging lava-monster? Because a solidly representative name and intriguing origin story will only do so much—ultimately, the most important factor in the *UPS* equation we discussed earlier is your costume. For instance, did you know that in today's image-obsessed culture, people make up their mind about you within fifteen seconds of meeting you face-to-face? That's *fifteen seconds, people!* When those fifteen seconds are up, the world should recognize you as an on-the-go hero who is not to be trifled with, rather than a slightly uncomfortable-looking guy in a too-small-for-his-face mask.

Of course, you've heard the story about the Flight Class hero who intervened in a burglary at the Museum of Ancient Antiquities only to be mistaken for a Super-Speed type. Naturally, she was mortified! But here's the part of the story you rarely hear: it was her costume that was responsible for the case of mistaken identity. Apparently, she'd insisted on using some lightning-bolt imagery for her insignia, and while yes, the long

vertical bolts had an overall slimming effect, what they said to the world was, "super-speed," not "flying." Which begs the questions:

What does *your* costume say about you?

What would you *like* it to say?

LEARNING TO LOVE THE WHOLE YOU

After months of working with a particularly problematic client, we had his costume looking spectacular. The sheer, smooth multi-fabric draped perfectly over his frame, while the combination sash/gliderchute (in fiery crimson Tightflex™) highlighted his trim waist and generously proportioned shoulders. But before I could even congratulate him, he turned to me with a frown. "We've got to do something about my pasty Rubberman neck," he mused. "Maybe we could chop it off?"

Ridiculous, right? Even though the costume was designed to call attention to his considerable assets (waist and shoulders), all this hero could see were his shortcomings. Unfortunately, too many of us (myself included) could tell this exact same story—with the only

HELPFUL HINT ALERT!
When changing out of your costume and back into your secret identity, remember to watch out for unsightly "mask-print"—not only can it be embarrassing, but those faint impressions left by your skintight mask or costume can lead others to guess your alter ego!

difference being that instead of a "pasty *Rubberman* neck," we complain about our *Geo-Beast* thighs or *Captain Zeppelin* butt. Why do we feel compelled to focus only on our bodies in negative terms? Here, for example, are a few of the things my clients have told me they particularly hate about themselves:

- "My hips are too big."
- "My boobs look funny."
- "My wings are *waaaay* too small. And they're on my ankles, for chrissake."
- "My skin is green, so whenever I wear red I look exactly like a shopping-mall elf. To make matters worse, under fluorescent light it takes on this very unflattering grayish-green hue."
- "These droopy gills of mine add about ten years. Thirteen, if I'm swimming in brackish water."
- "I *hate* my eyes. They used to be a nice brown color, but now they're perpetually charged with eighteen million terawatts of celestial energy, and the glow tends to wash out the rest of my features. Plus, I think not having discernible pupils freaks guys out."

Now I want you to add a few of your own:

- "I hate my _____."
- "My _____ are too big."
- "I wish my _____ were more like _____."

How did that feel? Familiar, right? In fact, I bet you had no problem filling in those blanks because this is what you do to yourself *all the time!* It pains me to watch otherwise strong, self-confident superheroes tearing themselves apart over a few perceived imperfections. This constant fixation on our so-called problems only invites hurtful negative energy into our lives—so starting today, I want you to stop obsessing over what's wrong with you and start to focus on all the things that are *right* with you! I'll get you started, OK? For example: "I love my hands. They're perfectly manicured yet still very masculine, and they discharge powerful bolts of primal energy from the fingertips."

Now it's your turn:

- "I *love* my _____."
- "I couldn't *live* without my _____."
- "My _____ are okay, *I suppose.*"

LET'S MEET . . . SEASONAL AFFECTIVE DISORDER!
Seasonal Affective Disorder, aka, SAD or "Sullen Footsoldier of the Winter Solstice," draws "its diabolical strength from the darkness and gloom of the winter months," "ruthlessly terrorizing the planet's inhabitants with lethargy, overeating, depression, and anxiety." A "fiendish monster," "who will stop at nothing until the world cowers beneath its cheerless gaze," SAD has also

been known to promote "irritability," "a decreased interest in crime-fighting," and even "death." Many a "normally well-adjusted hero" has been "found curled up on the couch," "totally bummed," and "compulsively listening to their REM albums" as a result of "SAD's disabling attacks." —from *Mister Mental's Survey of Supervillains,* 2003 edition

WHAT TYPE AM I?

Although we all carry our weight differently, and there's a good chance our superpowers have had varying distortive effects on our bodies, in general we all fall into one of four body types. For example, if your:

- Shoulders and torso are narrower than your hips, you are a *pear*. For you, we'll select dark fabrics that lengthen and flatter your upper body, while using epaulets or armor to fill out your frail shoulders. Avoid capes at all costs, as they will add about five inches (and several pounds) to your hips and thighs.

- Waist is narrow, but your shoulders and hips are roughly the same width, you are an *hourglass*. In your case, we'll be looking at soft, radiation-proof fabrics that you can layer to accentuate your natural curves. You may also want to look into a pair of knee-high (or higher) boots, in either leather or tritanium, to complement your legs and extend your body's contours.

- Shoulders and upper torso are wider than your hips, you are an *inverted triangle*. The sleek, tapering lines of your body mean you never have to be afraid of a skintight costume, and a cape will only enhance your generally dynamic air. To create definition around your waist, consider adding a utility belt or experimenting with some contrasting colors or bold patterns.

- Body exists only as an amorphous mass of energy or proto-plasm, you are a *gelatinous blob*. Since blobs, by definition, lack any consistent shape, your best bet will be to focus on finding those few perfect accessories that will really define your style. Perhaps a flirty scarf or an elegant set of nerve-bolts is just what you need to round out your new look!

DID YOU KNOW . . .

. . . that the first psionic heroes appeared on the battlefields of Western Europe and the Pacific during the latter part of 1944? Or that, by the end of World War II, Psionic Class heroes constituted nearly 10 percent of the active superhero population?

Almost overnight, it seemed, here they were: superheroes who could not only read minds and communicate telepathically, but who could, in some cases:

- Possess and manipulate other people (even other superheroes!)
- Create force fields and even crude implements of pure thought
- Generate vivid illusions and mental mirages
- Launch devastating psychic attacks such as cerebro-spikes, psi-bolts, and mind-storms
- Influence and control the physical world around them

In addition, the PCHs did not necessarily measure up to the superheroic standard. Whereas a chiseled physique, noble stature, and full head of magnificently flowing hair were once thought to be the norm, researchers now observed more than a few cases of male-pattern baldness, mild astigmatism, the occasional weak chin, and (most remarkable of all) physical handicaps sometimes requiring the use of a wheelchair or other assistive device.

COLOR: YOUR GREATEST ALLY . . . OR YOUR WORST NEMESIS?

Color is every hero's best friend. From the turquoise shimmer of an unfurled cape to the ruddy swagger of a super-speedster's crimson boots, superheroes have always turned to color to enhance authority, heighten mystery, or simply add that touch of magic that pulls an outfit together. Colors should not be treated lightly, however; much as they are the superhero's friend, they also have a dark side. As you'll see below, colors can be twisted, often against their will, and made to serve the powers of evil.

Color	When used for good, it's . . .	But in the hands of evil, it becomes the color of . . .
Red	The cozy glow of your heat vision; the healthy flush of your righteous anger; also, the color of fire trucks	Senseless bloodshed, arsonists, and Communism
Blue	Your coolly precise powers of deduction; the icy glow of your cosmic aura; the frigid blast of your ice-breath	Frostbite, depression, drowning
Green	The high-voltage radiance of your energy powers; the verdant lushness of the vegetation that obeys your commands; money for	Greed, envy, giant thunder lizards; also, money for radium weapons, henchman bonuses, and annoying gag gifts

	crimefighting gadgets and vehicles (also: ransoms)	
Yellow	The life-giving rays of the sun; the solar energy that recharges your amazing powers; vital traffic signs	Cowardice, pus
Black	A sensible reminder of the wages of sin; an executioner's hood	Evil's ultimate triumph over the forces of goodness and light

While even a semi-intelligent animal sidekick knows that bright colors *attract* evil and dark colors make it easier to *sneak up on* evil, if you really want to use color to help you express your UPS, you need to start by defining your seasonal color palette. What do I mean by this? Well, thanks to your meta-human chemistry, there are varying amounts of melanin, carotene, mutagens, and radioactive by-products in your skin and hair, meaning that certain colors will complement your features better than others. Try using the Personal Color Analyzer™ below to help you discover your very own seasonal palette.

PERSONAL COLOR ANALYZER™

Does your hair have golden, red, or fissile tones? Is it made from strands of cosmic fire? Do your eyes glow with an unearthly yellow or orange light?	*If you answered yes to any of these, you are an* → *If not, then . . .*	**Autumn** Autumns are vivid and often highly flammable. You love to fight crime in the late afternoon, when the sun make seven the battered face of your archenemy glow with a lush radiance
Is your skin the gorgeous green hue of enriched neutronium? Does it glow with the livid intensity of a bus-inflicted bruise? Do your powers involve the ability to manippastel or beige-colored energy?	*If you answered yes to any of these, you are a* → *If not, then . . .*	**Spring** Springs are energetic and radiant. You look best in half-masks and dominos of peach pink, golden yellow, and Kevlar. You love sheer fabrics and ulate indestructible alloys.
Is your hair actually a mass of cybernetically controlled invincium fibers? Is your skin plated with some sort	*If you answered yes to any of these, you are a* → *If not, then . . .*	**Winter** Winters are forceful and profound. You look best in icy, vivid colors such as black,

of highly reflective metal armor? Are your powers related to the underworld or otherwise supernatural?		white, and depleted uranium.
Does your hair have ultraviolet or fluoronic highlights? Does your skin burn with the radiance of the sun? Do you possess the almighty power of the atom?	*If you answered yes to any of these, you are a* ⟶	**Summer** Summers are sultry and often fiercely radioactive. You look best in tones (like charred-flesh black, running-sore yellow, and mushroom-cloud grey) that won't fight for attention with your natural coloring.

DISCOVERING YOUR PERSONAL STYLE

What sort of costume is right for you? The following quiz will help you find out. Once you add up your score and identify your personal style, use the following wardrobe descriptions to help plan your next shopping trip!

1. Let's say that Thermostatix has hijacked InterCorp's new intrinsic thermal amplifier and is on his way to the North Pole in his Magma-Mobile to melt the ice cap and turn the eastern seaboard into the world's biggest wading pool. What would you wear while thwarting this insidious plot?

a) A simple, sleek one-piece in a bold color; knee-high boots with a radiation-proof sole; and a no-cling cape perfectly tailored to my heroic figure

b) Fitted bottoms made from a Spandex-tritanium 50/50 blend; a vivid, skin-tight top that's guaranteed to dazzle against the cool tones of the arctic landscape; mittens

c) A rapid-deployment arctic-ready exo-suit, with holographic camouflaging capabilities, ram-jet–powered snowshoes, and a large-caliber freeze ray

d) The traditional garb of the hardy Inuit people

2. Complete this sentence: "If I could only use one crime-fighting accessory for the rest of my life, it would have to be . . ."

a) My amazing power ring

b) My silken cord and collapsible grappling hook

c) My amply stocked utility belt

d) My .50-caliber semiautomatic Desert Eagle pistol, which I playfully refer to as "The Throb-matic Love-Plunger"

3. What time of day do you prefer to fight crime?

a) Afternoon

b) Early morning

c) Midnight to 4 a.m.

d) Anytime my alien cells can easily absorb the rays of your yellow sun

4. Which of the following best describes your attitude toward supervillains?

a) Most evil-doers would respond nicely to a little group therapy and a 12-step program of some sort

b) A vigorous lobotomizing is all that's needed to help them become productive members of society

c) "Tough love"—by which I mean grinding their faces into rain-slicked, blood-spattered asphalt until they go limp and crap in their pants

5. What is the most important room in your secret headquarters?

a) The "danger room"—because constant honing of my superpowers is the key to a long and successful career

b) The "trophy room"—because the bizarre memorabilia of my adventures might be worth something someday

c) The "neural nexus chamber"—because a sentient supercomputer is crucial if I want to stay one step ahead of my crafty archnemesis

d) The "rumpus room"—because it's got air hockey!

6. How do you prefer to be alerted to a crisis or emergency?

a) Flashing red phone

b) Insignia projected against the night sky

c) Hypersonic alert beacon

d) Hearsay; unsubstantiated rumor

7. What is your preferred mode of transportation?

a) Self-propelled (i.e., flying, super-speed, super-leaps, etc.)

b) Advanced, state-of-the-art crimefighting mobile

c) Leaping from rooftop to rooftop in a stirring display of agility and daring

d) Bumming a ride from friends; walking

8. You would like others to perceive you as:

a) A shining beacon of truth and justice

    b) A noble warrior guided by virtue and honor
    c) A dark symbol of vengeance and retribution
    d) The pickle-eating champion of the universe

9. Which colors, textures, and materials dominate your wardrobe?
    a) Bold, bright hues and energy-absorbing fabrics
    b) Frictionless ceramic-titanium blends and form-lengthening patterns
    c) Dark, authoritative tones, Prilex™ exo-armor, and radar-invisible carbon weaves
    d) Fun, flirty colors and lightweight cotton prints

10. How would you describe your current costume?
    a) Clean, bright, a symbol of who I am and what I stand for
    b) Industrial, utilitarian, frequently lethal
    c) Armored, impenetrable, non-floating
    d) Deadly alien symbiote

EVALUATING YOUR SCORE

To calculate your score, first assign each of your answers a numerical equivalent:

    a) = 1; b) = 2; c) = 3; d) = 4

Now, add up your score and then use the following profiles to learn more about your style type:

    32–24: You are a *Modern/Trendy*
    23–16: You are a *Sporty*
    15–8: You are a *Classic*

CLASSIC

If you're a Classic, you're always on the prowl for those simple, timeless fashions that form the building blocks of your look. Eschewing trends, you seek out the understated and the elegant, the tried and the true. Classic styles dress up easily, so you can go from a frenzied battle with your archfoe to a night on the town in just a few minutes. You use accessories sparingly. You have an irrational hatred of paisley.

THREE THINGS EVERY CLASSIC HERO
SHOULD HAVE IN HIS OR HER CLOSET:

1. Sleek bodysuit made of PlaSkin™ or other synthetic fiber. This item—formfitting but *never* clingy—is a must-have for any superhero.

2. Dressy, Flexi-Steel™ top with cap sleeves and omni-probing nano-circuitry. A seasonless top that you'll want to wear whether confronting interdimensional apocalypse or just lounging around. (Note: Heroines may also substitute a lightly armored WonderLift™ demi-bra.)

3. Full-body microfiber cloak, tailored to hang just below the ankle. This style can look a bit frumpy on anyone other than a Magus Class hero, but in a dark or neutral color it can absolutely *make* an outfit.

SPORTY

If your friends and teammates often describe your wardrobe as "exciting," "vivacious," and "slutty," then there's little doubt that you're a Sporty. You love the freedom and flexibility of the new synthetics—particularly the "ultra" fabrics—and you're not afraid to "mix things up" with some adventurous accessories. Sporty types emphasize mobility over modesty (i.e., flashing a bit of thigh or baring some midriff while dishing out a "Ka-pow" or a "Blamm-o" bothers you not in the least). You favor bold colors.

THREE THINGS EVERY SPORTY HERO SHOULD HAVE IN HIS OR HER CLOSET:

> **HELPFUL HINT ALERT!**
> Though some fabrics—like ultra-suede or Nomex—will work with almost any costume, one should never attempt to fight evil while wearing any of the following:
>
> - Flannel
> - Gingham
> - Tweed
> - Naugahyde

1. Skimming, low-waisted jumpsuit bottoms with anti-grav piping along the outer seam. These skintight yet always-flattering bottoms will minimize your tummy and make you look lightning-fast (even if you're only waiting in line at Starbucks).
2. Long-sleeved, form-fitting crewneck shirt in ultra-mesh or NU-fiber. Perfect for casual crimefighting or reconnaissance, this shirt's shaped, retro chic will give you plenty of street cred.
3. Knee-high syntho-skin boots with a Type 3 tritanium shell and Vibram soles. No matter what kind of butt you have to kick, these boots will make sure you look fabulous doing it. (Note: Heroines may want to opt for fishnet stockings as well as the more obviously impractical stiletto heel.)

MODERN/TRENDY

You were the first superhero in your city to own a stealth cowl. You had a pair of fly quantum-knit mega-slacks before anyone else even knew what they were. And you were coolly vaporizing evil-doers with your dissolvo-vision long before the "hard-core" thing was cool. Why? Because you're Modern/Trendy, and you can no more stop living on the cutting edge of superhero fashion than you can stop blaming yourself for what happened to Los Angeles.

**THREE THINGS EVERY MODERN/TRENDY HERO
SHOULD HAVE IN HIS OR HER CLOSET:**

1. Experimental exo-suit with dropped waist and optional ram-jet package. Hearts will beat faster and jaws will drop as you flash down the avenues in pursuit of wickedness while wearing this impervious yet breathable body armor.

2. Full-body "smart" coat, knee-cut and handwoven from organic steel. After one glimpse of you in this slightly boxy, *very* sexy trench-styled coat, your archenemy won't be able to escape you—even in his dreams.

3. Nano-armor. An impenetrable network of microscopic buckyballs that coats your entire body and is directly linked to the bioelectric field generated by your super fashion sense. The instant you recognize a stylish new trend, the multifaceted spheres rotate to reveal a new color or texture, instantly updating your look and keeping you solidly in the vanguard of gorgeousness. (Note: Heroines may choose to substitute crotchless panties.)

Masks, Capes, and Utility Belts

At this point, you should be well on your way toward a UPS that answers the question posed to you at the beginning of this chapter: *Who are you?* Just as an artist works in mediums such as clay, oils, or urine-soaked religious icons, so have you wrought from your name, origin story, and personal style a more profound, precise rendering of yourself. But before we move on to the next chapter, let's put the finishing touches on the new *you* with a few carefully-chosen *accessories*.

When it comes to accessorizing, less is usually more. We've all seen superheroes who push it too far—mixing a heavy, cowled cape with a visored helmet and power gauntlets, for example—and end up looking cheap or even silly. The key is to choose accessories that complement your overall look while subtly drawing attention to your best features. For example:

> **HELPFUL HINTS**
>
> Do you wear exo-armor or a battlesuit? If so, then you know how tough it can be to keep it smelling fresh, particularly after a long, sweaty day of tackling evil. So next time, try placing some potpourri or a sprig of mint in the heel of your anti-grav boots, and enjoy a clean, springtime scent all day long!

- Love your hips and thighs? Then a bulky utility belt, worn just below the navel, might be the answer.
- Do your hands belong in the Louvre? Modern weaponry—particularly some of the more striking alien designs—can often double for visually interesting jewelry. Try a pair of force bracelets or null-manacles to help keep those hands front-and-center.

- Do your eyes have special superpowers of their own? Masks are not only a great way to keep your secret identity a *secret,* but they're also perfect for calling attention to those darling peepers. A word of caution, however: if you have dark eyes, choose a mask in neutral colors; if your eyes are lighter, you should select a shade that will enhance their natural brilliance.
- Power rings and magic amulets not only are a great way to harness a vast array of mind-boggling superpowers, but when used properly, they can show off your mind-boggling natural assets, too!

THE MANHATTAN GAMBIT

"In 1946, the head of the Manhattan Project, Dr. Morbius, fearing that his funding would be cut as part of the 'peace dividend,' convinced the House Committee on Meta-Humans that the emergence of a new enemy—Red Communism—could only be deterred through the development of increasingly advanced and powerful superheroes.

"With a thoroughly terrified Congress in his pocket, the only significant obstacle faced by Morbius was the American people. Absent the unifying threat of world war, the public was no longer quite so willing to lend their bodies and minds to the oft-disfiguring cause of meta-human advancement. This represented a problem for Dr. Morbius, though not, apparently, an insurmountable one.

"Close scrutiny of the safety records of the various Manhattan Project facilities (including the subaquatic *Meridian Complex*), between the years 1948 and 1959, reveals a regular increase in

the number of accidents suffered by Manhattan Project employees. Of course, these 'accidents' were actually experiments conducted by Dr. Morbius to test various theories of meta-human
development on unsuspecting scientists, research assistants, and
janitors.

"Dr. Morbius's first success occurred at exactly 7:21 on the
morning of October 10, 1949. Struck by a stasis disruptor's
quantum flare as he was pushing his fiancée from its path, Professor Buzz Brant received a dose of elemental radiation comparable to that released by an Omegatronic bomb. This sudden
massive energy bombardment triggered a series of dramatic
cellular mutations, mutations which enabled Professor Brant to
transform from a sickly human into the fantastically strong,
iron-skinned creature now known as *Helter-Smelter.*" —from
*Betrayal of Trust: The Secret War of Dr. Klaus
Rudolph Morbius,* by Richard W. Lobel

Chapter Eleven

Finding Your Ideal Secret Headquarters in Any Real Estate Market

"I'm just not sure what you want me to do for you," I said, flipping through the album of newspaper and magazine clippings he'd thrust in front of me. I turned the page to a story from the *Sioux City Clipper,* headlined, "Local Hero Takes Home High Honor." I didn't bother to read the article, but I did glance at the photo long enough to confirm that the man in front of me was, in fact, the same "local hero." His costume was a little faded in some places, the edges of his mask a little threadbare, but aside from that, it was him. *Headstrong.* The Battering Man. Nominated for "The Most Promising New Superhero" at the 1998 IBSH Awards. The Pride of Sioux City.*

And he needed my help.

"I don't know exactly how it started," he was saying. "Everything was going great. It even looked like some of the local supervillains were going to team up and form an LLEC† just to try and defeat me. But then, I don't know, all these little things

---

*This precedes the events of the Crossverse Crisis, during which Sioux City was miniaturized and placed in an empty Gallo wine jug.
†Limited-Liability Evil Corporation

started happening. Like, the Head-Signal would go off and I'd race out to the Omnimobile . . . only it's not there. And I'm thinking, did Minefield steal it? Did the Invisible Shark vaporize it? No. Turns out the wife borrowed it to take the kids to soccer practice. So I had to drive the minivan. And I don't have to tell you how *that* looks.

"And there're other things. Like the tracer I secretly planted on a high-level L.I.M.P. operative. The one that didn't work because my daughter took the batteries for her Game Boy. Or the time I caught my oldest using the interwave transcoder to pull down the Spice Channel. And then there's, you know, a man gets tired of blowing a fuse every time he's using his supercomputer and someone microwaves a burrito."

I couldn't believe what I was hearing. "Let me get this straight: you don't have a secret HQ*? You're still working out of your *home?*"

The Battering Man just looked at me. "Is that bad?" he asked.

Now, the point of me telling this story is not to poke fun at Headstrong, whose career, by the way, I was able to turn around after just a few consultations. Rather, I use it to illustrate one of the biggest mistakes that new heroes can make: not investing in a fully functional secret headquarters.

*Secret headquarters; also, SHQ

"DO I REALLY NEED A SECRET HQ?"

Remember how the Internet was going to enable superheroes to "telecommute" from their homes, thus eliminating the need for secret HQs altogether? Ironically, just the opposite has happened. Over the past few years we've seen more and more heroes returning to their orbiting base stations, subterranean caverns, and elegant mansions. The reasons for this, while numerous, nonetheless suggest that the well-concealed home base is still an essential part of a successful superheroic career. For example, a secret HQ means:

- Ample storage space—you'll finally be able to rescue that particle accelerator from your parents' basement
- Lots of built-in shelving so you can get organized and rid yourself of unsightly "gadget clutter"
- Thick, tritanium-fused concrete walls that offer instant relief from even the most lethal radiological attacks
- A secluded or hard-to-reach location that offers plenty of time for personal reflection (i.e., brooding, stewing, endlessly revisiting gory flashbacks, etc.)
- Cedar-lined closets that are perfect for "modified costume" storage—the fresh woodsy scent will keep your underwater, interplanetary, and arctic adventure costumes ready for action (also ideal for storing delicates such as cashmere knits or poly-stealth blends)
- Your very own VTOL- and helicopter-ready landing pad that retracts into a mountainside for easy concealment and out-of-the-way storage

- A subterranean, steel-reinforced patio with laser turret, escape tunnel, and unobstructed views of stalagmites, bats, and blind salamanders

"WHAT KIND OF SECRET HQ IS RIGHT FOR ME?"

Right about now is when most superheroes, seemingly bewitched by terms like "ion pulse cannon" and "molecular destabilization ray," and desperate for a subterranean escape pod of their very own, run out and grab the first secret headquarters they can find. But why is this a mistake? After all, didn't I just tell you that you *needed* a secret headquarters? Well, yes, but not just *any* secret headquarters. Whichever one you choose, chances are that you're going to be making it your base of operations for the next several years. By taking the time now to be sure you're making the right choice, you can ensure that those years will be happy, productive, and free from expensive force-field repairs or costly system upgrades.

LET'S MEET . . . THE WINGED BRAIN!
While most heroes seem to agree that the Winged Brain ("rhymes with 'learned'") is "not really the best adversary to face if you've been out drinking the night before," a few insist that "you haven't really battled evil until you've fought a renegade telekinetic brain with wings." Formerly known as Captain Dirk

Mayday, a "famed aviator, adventurer, and world-class brain scientist" who "curiously insisted on maintaining his experimental laboratory in the same hangar as his squadron of modified Hawker Hurricanes," he "pretty much got what he asked for when a propeller cut him to pieces and his brain ended up in a vat of his extra-strength neurofluid." Though even fans admit that the details of how the wings came about are "a little sketchy," there's no doubt that the Winged Brain "is thoroughly obsessed with the notion that the world's leaders are controlled by a highly placed pair of Old Navy cargo pants" and is "as we speak probably creating an army of winged monkey brains to help him carry out his plans for world domination."　　—from *Mister Mental's Survey of Supervillains,* 2004 edition

The following simple "fill-in-the-blank" statements will help you focus on what to keep in mind when shopping around for a *sanctum sanctorum.* Remember, you don't want to lose sight of your priorities and become infatuated with an appealing but costly add-on such as a self-destruct mechanism. And be sure to write down your answers—they'll serve as a handy guide while you're searching for that perfect place to call a fully automated, state-of-the-art defense fortress of your own.

- My ideal secret headquarters has _____ (*number*) rooms.
- My ideal secret headquarters is located in _____ (*the city, the suburbs, the fifth dimension, The Shadow Zone, suborbital space, etc.*).

- My ideal secret headquarters is powered by a(n) _____ _____ (*lava mill, atomic reactor, antimatter stack, N5 fusion bubble, etc.*).
- My ideal secret headquarters is close to _____ (*shopping, good schools, a transdimensional wormhole, etc.*).
- If my secret headquarters could have one special feature, it would be a(n) _____ (*sentient computer, alien zoo, herb garden/home theater, etc.*).
- I plan to use my secret headquarters primarily for _____ _____ (*entertaining, self-defense, storage, honing my powers, brooding, etc.*).

However, there are still a few things you need to understand before you rush out and plunk down a sizeable chunk of your savings on a new lair. First, not all secret HQs are going to be right for all superheroes—there's no such thing as a one-size-fits-all crimefighting retreat. For example, maybe you've always dreamed of a modern operations center with a giant plasma vidscreen, second-generation matter analyzer, and charming breakfast nook. Or perhaps you have more traditional tastes, in which case you might picture yourself operating out of a dormant volcano, complete with a flight elevator, telescoping extraction claws, and oodles of closet space. No matter what style you're in the market for, from colonial to contemporary, you'll find that today's headquarters-minded hero has never had more choices. Some of the more popular secret headquarters designs include:

THE "RUSTIC"

For superheroes who value their privacy, frequently find themselves persecuted by intolerant humans, or simply crave some "alone time," the Rustic-style headquarters offers an irresistible combination of solitude and fully networked, multiphase atomic nullifiers. Often embedded in an arctic wasteland, dormant volcano, subterranean cavern, or alpine peak, or in some cases part of a mysterious "floating" island, the Rustic-style base manages to reflect the unique spirit of its bleak surroundings while still offering all the charm and highly destructive firepower you've come to expect from today's secluded super-fortress.

THE "CLASSIC"

As its name might imply, the Classic-style headquarters blends Old World sophistication with state-of-the-art evil-suppression technology. Though often referred to as "stately manors" or "ancestral castles," almost any type of Westchester mansion, Apex City townhouse, or Sloverian medieval fortress may legitimately be characterized as a Classic-style base of operations. Note: Despite the argument that these mansions or castles are simply facades for what is essentially a contemporary subterranean base, the term continues to be recognized by the BMHA.

THE "CONTEMPORARY"

The Contemporary secret headquarters was created to help today's surperhero meet the many, often conflicting demands of modern evil-smashing. Founded on the principles of Big Science design, this base of operations combines all the convenience and firepower you expect in a headquarters with the utility and impregnability of a traditional secret fortress. Available in a range of styles, from orbiting to sub-dimensional, with up to ten different levels to choose from, including a crime-lab option, danger room/family fitness package, vehicle docking bay, tactical command center, and mystical energies vortex.

THE "MOBILE"

For those frustrated by the relative immovability of most secret headquarters, and willing to sacrifice amenities like subterranean levels or hidden runways in favor of flexibility and speed, a Mobile base of operations might make sense. Mobile headquarters are designed to travel on land, through the air, beneath the sea, or even between dimensions. They can be anything from an armored van with its own dashboard-mounted tactical center and sonic battering ram to a heli-carrier, stealth blimp, or jet-sub. (Author's note: Concerning space-based headquarters, any base locked in geosynchronous orbit is considered "fixed," while a base that's capable of movement would be categorized as "Mobile.")

THE "INDUSTRIAL"

One of the more modern headquarters designs, the Industrial-style base is typically sited among the picturesque brownfields and charming urban blight that surround most large cities. Favored mainly by Crimefighter Class heroes who have chosen to immerse themselves in a gritty, ultraviolent environment, these locales typically feature meta-human street gangs and plenty of criminal scum. This design is unique among hidden base layouts in that it eschews such "standard" features as escape pods and evil-tracking multi-signal arrays in favor of homemade booby traps, freight elevators, and *noir* atmosphere.

LET'S MEET . . . BLINDSIDE!
A "funky," "unpretentious," but "often annoyingly stoned" supervillain, Blindside was "an up-and-coming extreme sports competitor and bike messenger" until the day he was "sideswiped by a taxi," "did a totally gnarly endo," and "pancaked on top of his Manhattan Portage bag," shattering the vials of experimental chemicals he was transporting for InterMech Corporation. The chemicals entered his bloodstream "through a freshly pierced nipple," unexpectedly reacting with "his Pabst Blue Ribbon–soaked physiology" and "granting him superhuman speed and reflexes." Though his "lack of initiative" can be "frustrating," his "arsenal of modified extreme sports equipment" and "colorful vocabulary" make "foiling this supervillain a real treat." Overall, he "could be a substantial threat if he ever moves out of his parents' garage." —from *Mister Mental's Survey of Supervillains,* 2001 supplemental

---

The One Thing No Secret HQ Can Be Without

People often ask me, "Doctor Metropolis, what's the most important thing to keep in mind when shopping for a secret headquarters?" And unlike other questions I often get,* this one's easy. The answer, of course, is *location, location, location!*

---

*Such as, "Who would win in a fight, Helter-Smelter or Dr. Shellfish?"

Specifically, this means you want to establish yourself in an area with a *high crime rate.* This is key. Many first-time HQ renters or buyers overlook this essential factor, and yet it is *the* single most important thing to consider when choosing a head-quarters. Imagine how frustrating it would be to move into a se-cret headquarters in a nice neighborhood only to find yourself spending hours commuting back and forth to high-crime areas!

Also keep in mind that you're looking for a specific kind of villainy. You didn't become a superhero to foil so-called crimes such as postal fraud, noise pollution, or vehicular homicide. Rather, you're going to be focusing on neighborhoods that have a high incidence of elaborate jewel heists, armored car hijack-ings, and diabolical attempts at world domination. Check with the police department in the area you're considering moving to in order to learn more about local evil-doers. (Note: Approach police while in your secret identity, not as a costumed vigilante). And visit the neighborhood yourself—you can learn a lot through simple observation!

Here are some of the telltale signs of possible supervillain activity:

- Killer robots loitering outside the Dairy Queen
- Area merchants that cater to a supervillain clientele (i.e., death-ray repairmen, robo-hound kennels, evil henchmen temp agencies, etc.)
- No greeters at local Wal-Mart
- Packs of wild dogs roaming freely through mall
- Mutants, zombies, and CHUDs constitute significant voting bloc
- You keep hearing faint but unmistakable sound of maniacal laughter
- Junk mail addressed to "Evil Occupant"
- Flying monkeys

RENT VS. OWN

There is no right or wrong answer to the question of renting vs. buying. Which solution is right for you depends on your personality, your wallet, and your long-term goals. In fact, the same hero may choose different options at different points in his or her career. While it's up to you, I believe that if you're a young, first-time hero, or if you've been given the opportunity to become a superhero at a more mature stage of your life, it often makes sense to rent until you're certain that the superhero lifestyle is really something you want.

- Blockbuster employees insist on addressing each customer as "my Dark Lord"
- Garage sales feature unusual concentration of bargain-priced doomsday beams, alchemy pistols, and gently used brain scramblers

"HOW DO I FIND SECRET HQS THAT ARE FOR SALE?"

Who knows how many superheroes have had trouble sorting through the arcane, confusing language of secret headquarters listings, but were too proud to pick up the phone and ask for help? While I can't change the real estate industry, I can help you understand the rules of the game, beginning with the following translations of some *actual* secret headquarters listings. I hope you find them useful.

A good example of an Industrial-style secret HQ, circa 1964.

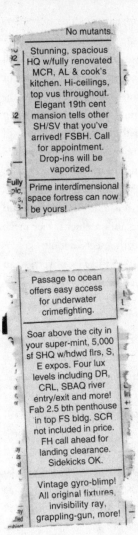

No mutants.

Stunning, spacious HQ w/fully renovated MCR, AL & cook's kitchen. Hi-ceilings, top vus throughout. Elegant 19th cent mansion tells other SH/SV that you've arrived! FSBH. Call for appointment. Drop-ins will be vaporized.

Prime interdimensional space fortress can now be yours!

A good example of a Classic-style headquarters will probably be a little out of your price range if you're like most new heroes, but the fact that the ad doesn't mention location means it might be in a decent neighborhood, which should give you a little more bargaining power.

MCR=master/multi-command room, AL=airlock, SH/SV= superhero/supervillain, FSBH=for sale by hero

Passage to ocean offers easy access for underwater crimefighting.

Soar above the city in your super-mint, 5,000 sf SHQ w/hdwd flrs, S, E expos. Four lux levels including DR, CRL, SBAQ river entry/exit and more! Fab 2.5 bth penthouse in top FS bldg. SCR not included in price. FH call ahead for landing clearance. Sidekicks OK.

Vintage gyro-blimp! All original fixtures, invisibility ray, grappling-gun, more!

For purposes of defense as well as concealment, most secret headquarters tend to be underground, but that's not always the best option for Flight Class heroes or those who travel by swinging or leaping from building to building. Such heroes may find this lofty base ideal, and well worth the premium price.

SHQ=secret headquarters, DR= danger room, CRL=crime lab, SBAQ=subaquatic, SCR– supercomputer, FH=Flight Class hero

Clearly a fixer-upper, this secret headquarters could require anywhere from a few thousand to several million dollars' worth of renovations before you'll feel confident that the outer shields will be able to withstand the five million kilotons/psi (or in practical terms, the equivalent of one of *Count Fusion*'s nova-blasts) that's required by most state and local inspection boards. However, if you're not afraid of a little hard work, then the outstanding location and (most likely) bargain-basement price make this property worth a second look.

BDR=blast doors, STLTH=subterranean tunnel leading to helipad

Asking the Right Questions

Let's say you find a secret headquarters that seems perfect. Not only is it in a community with a good school system, but it's close to both a supervillain rehab center (supervillains are notoriously incorrigible) and a top-secret military weapons lab. Should you act fast and sign a contract right away?

Absolutely not! Before you put any money down, you need to do a little more research. While the owner is not obligated to volunteer information about any defects in the property, he is required to truthfully answer any questions you may have. Some good ones to start with are:

- "Do any supervillains know of this base's secret location?"
- "Is there a self-destruct mechanism installed on the property? If so, has it been activated?"
- "Do you know of any alien super-race that has currently targeted this secret headquarters for destruction?"
- "Have you ever had any problems with flooding?" (Note: This will mainly be of concern to superheroes based in the Northeast and Midwest.)
- "Is it haunted?"

"CAN I ADD A SECRET HEADQUARTERS TO MY EXISTING HOME?"

Whether you live in a cozy studio apartment or a grand sixteen-bedroom estate with private drive and eat-in Jacuzzi, adding a secret headquarters to your residence is a great do-it-yourself project that adds privacy, value, and security to your home. Whether you're considering a full-size underground complex with ultra-modern crimefighting appliances, or are just looking to upgrade an existing space using found objects, some throw pillows, and a small molecular transporter, you'll find that this is a project that will delight and inspire for years to come.

But of course, as with any ambitious home-improvement project, and particularly one that involves the handling and disposal of anti-matter waste, you will face challenges. For starters, the majority of residences simply aren't designed to accommodate even the most basic superhero amenities. Just bringing the electrical wiring up to code could cost tens of thousands of dollars.

You also may be assuming that any home improvements you

HELPFUL HINT ALERT!

One way to help reduce the stress and confusion of shopping for a secret headquarters is to use a real estate agent. However, not all agents are alike, so here are a few things you should keep in mind when selecting one:

- Be sure they have experience working with superheroes. Your requirements will be quite different from those of other clients. Look for someone who understands and can help satisfy those special needs.
- Ask your agent if they have any psionic abilities or mind-control implants. Agents are required by law to disclose this information to you, since it could adversely affect any negotiations you might enter into with them.
- Today's high-pressure super-agent is often tomorrow's tyrannical world dictator—that's right, it's possible that your agent has evil tendencies or is already a supervillain! While this may turn out to be a good thing, as it means your agent will be willing to lie, cheat, and even kill in order to put you in your ideal secret headquarters, it's still something you'll probably want to know about beforehand.

THE FIVE MOST POPULAR SECRET HEADQUARTERS "DO-IT-YOURSELF" PROJECTS

According to a 2004 Home Depot study, these are the most popular renovation projects for superheroes who are adding or fixing up a secret headquarters:

1. Transforming the basement into a "rumpus room/danger room" (heroes can challenge their colleagues to a game of bumper pool or opt to hone their powers against an endless variety of holographic foes)
2. Enlarging the kitchen so that one's faithful manservant or butler has more room to prepare nourishing finger sandwiches
3. Replacing the ancient CRT monitors in the command center with sleek HDTV plasma screens and ear-rattling 5:1 Bose surround-sound
4. Expanding the library to accommodate a fake bookshelf that, with the touch of a hidden switch, slides away to reveal poles that lead to the heart of the subterranean base
5. Installing an underground runway complete with holographically shielded entrance

make will automatically increase your home's value. However, many of the alterations essential to a smoothly functioning secret headquarters—such as gigantic, evil-detecting antennae or an above-ground pool—could actually hurt your home's all-important resale value. Similarly, if you live in a planned suburban development, your homeowners' association will likely frown on additions such as a launching pad for your crusading rocket-car or a steel Defens-o-dome, arguing that such improvements clash with the neighborhood's carefully contrived faux-Tudor milieu.

A Successful Base of Operations Renovation

What a difference an all-purpose power beam makes! As these before-and-after pictures vividly demonstrate, Headstrong, whom you met at the beginning of this chapter (remember, he was the one going crazy trying to fight crime out of his home?), was able to transform his plain, 1950s ranch-style house into a smart, distinctive, and fully operational secret headquarters accented with "Big Science" flair (see *Figure 2-1*). Read on to learn more about how he pulled off this remarkable transformation— maybe you'll be inspired to tackle a home-improvement project of your own!

Before

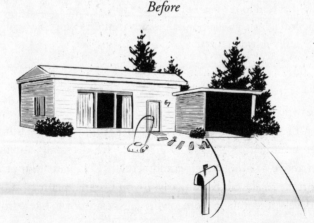

After

Figure 2-1

- "We loved our dining room's arched doorway and decorative moldings," explained Headstrong's wife, Eve, "but we were afraid that they'd lose some of their impact once we raised the ceiling to make room for the solid-light accelerator." Ultimately, they were able to preserve the room's classic personality by eliminating the ceiling altogether, installing an electromagnetic iris, and running a catwalk around the perimeter of the room for access.

- Despite the fact that Headstrong and Eve had just finished off their basement a few years before in order to create a separate space for their kids, both their nine-year-old and six-year-old continued to spend most of their time in the family room. "They never really took to it," admitted the hardheaded hero. So when he finally had the chance to gut the basement and extend it down another four floors, plus create an underground hanger for his twin-jet, everyone was happy with the result.

- Before the renovation, whenever Headstrong would need to temporarily incarcerate a supervillain while awaiting a BMHA retrieval team, he would have to bring them in through the laundry room. "It was the quickest route to the stasis containment cylinder, but I just hated the thought that one of them might see my Victoria's Secret 'Such a Flirt' panties as they went by," confessed Eve, "to say nothing of [Headstrong's] spare costume!" So after getting a special permit, the Battering Man had a slip-tube installed that went directly from the curb to the new Level 3 containment field. Voilà—no more dirty crooks eyeing the dirty laundry!

BRAVE NEW WORLD

"Manhattan Project scientists achieved two key national security goals during the 1960s. First, they strategically placed mutation-promoting chemicals and radioactive waste near population centers and military bases throughout North America; and second, they engineered eighteen new meta-humans—the first TCHs. Obsessed with the need to create an aura of legitimacy for his creations, Dr. Morbius (with the quiet backing of the government) maneuvered to gain control of the Valaxis Society's governing body, referred to as the *Archeon*. He ultimately succeeded, and officially designated a new power class for his mutant heroes (the Transmutation Class). However, his machinations were uncovered, and in the resulting scandal, more than half the society's member heroes resigned.

"At almost the same time, the *Forest Hills Massacre* occurred. A few days later, in Galveston, Texas, the Flight Class hero known as the *Silver Seraph* was beaten to death by an angry mob (he had been temporarily grounded, having damaged his wings during the *Excellion Invasion*). A group of more than three thousand superheroes marched on Washington in protest. Public reaction was fiercely divided. Events appeared to be reaching a critical mass.

"Finally, the Nixon administration, recognizing the very real possibility that the Trats (a class of superhero that represented a substantial government investment) might become so disaffected by the ongoing public persecution and outright racism that they would take some extreme action, stepped in to quiet the growing civil unrest. Most significantly, they pushed the *Goldberg-Soeiro Act* through Congress. This legislation created the Bureau of Meta-Human Affairs, a federal agency charged with the oversight, regulation, and administration of all meta-humans, active and nonactive, in the United States and its territories."   —from
Prejudice Unmasked: Anti-Hero Backlash During the Postwar Years, by R. A. Sillett

Chapter Twelve

Choosing the Archenemy That's Right for You

There comes a time in every superhero's life when you wake up and realize that something's missing. All of a sudden, the things you'd found so fulfilling—pummeling supervillains, participating in secret wars, sacrificing your life to save the universe—aren't enough. It's as if one day you looked around and it seemed like everyone but you had found that "special evil someone" to share their life with.

Does this mean it's too late for you? That you're destined to spend the rest of your life battling low-level thugs and lame super-foes like *Professor Absorbo* or *Mister Blister?* Not at all, for in this chapter I'm going to teach you how to:

- Discover what sort of archenemy is right for you
- Attract and land the nemesis of your dreams
- Build a lasting, hostile, mutually abusive superhero-supervillain relationship
- Communicate difficult feelings

ALL ARCHENEMIES ARE *NOT* CREATED EQUAL

What are you looking for in an archenemy? Most heroes just have a vague sense that they want to be with someone really evil, but that description covers a lot of territory. For example, is your ideal nemesis someone who enjoys taunting you by leaving a trail of grisly riddles? Or is it someone who will murder your loved ones just to get your attention? Does your taste in archfiends run to those who will try to mystically switch bodies with you? Or are you looking for someone who will lure you into an impossibly elaborate deathtrap involving mutant teddy bears and lots of jagged edges?

In order to help you become more familiar with the various types of archenemies, I've compiled this comprehensive breakdown of nemesis types, the result of four incredibly tedious years spent studying more than 2,500 superhero/supervillain relationships.

The Masked Loser

Also known as: the Temp, Mr. Small-Time, Underachiever, Minor League, Work-in-Process, Stool Pigeon, Idiot, Mindless Cretin

Advantages: Easily satisfied; low-maintenance; always up for a good beating

Disadvantages: Lacks ambition, higher brain processes; still a small-time crook at heart; no matter how spectacular his powers he continues to focus on bank robberies, counterfeiting, piracy on the high seas, etc.; may drag you down to his level

Often heard saying: "Fools! No mere tritanium vault can withstand my *power!* The Jewel of Bachus will soon be *mine!*"

XL-9000

Also known as: Colecovision, the Six-Million-Dollar Dud, Loser-Bot, Tin Man, Mr. Does-Not-Compute, Lame-iac

Advantages: Typically a super-intelligent computer or android with loads of cool technology (like a time machine) and weapons (like lasers); exhibits genocidal disdain for "flesh-creatures"; ability to control all forms of technology a major plus

Disadvantages: May freeze up if required to process multiple evil commands simultaneously; easily stumped by paradoxical, Zen koan–type questions; constantly requires upgrade to latest version of evil; inability to comprehend mysteries of the human heart leads to oft-paralyzing confusion; prone to rust

Often heard saying: "No! That . . . does not *compute!* I cannot be defeated by a mere *human!* That is . . . *illogical!!*"

Mr. Omnipotent

Also known as: the Mighty Blowhard, Ye Olde Crackpot, More-Pompous-Than-Thou, the Cranky One, Mrs. Doubtfire

Advantages: Often wields powers far beyond your comprehension; thinks nothing of destroying or consuming a planet (usually *your* planet); will gamble with the lives of millions in casual wagers with other omnipotent beings

Disadvantages: Immortality leads to procrastination on a galactic scale; rarely actually gets around to destroying anything; appears to be making up laws of universe as he goes along; awfully easy to outwit for someone who's supposed to know everything

Often heard saying: "You think your puny powers can harm me? Me, son of the cosmos and heir to apocalypse? I, who exist beyond all knowledge and understanding? I, who stand astride the galaxies and drink deep of the sweet, sugary vastness of space? I, who can snuff out entire solar systems with just a thought? I, who . . ." etc., etc.

The Boss
Also known as: Mr. Big, the Big Boss, Bossy McBoss, the Bosster, Boss-zilla, Boss Hogg, Tubby

Advantages: Holds sway over massive criminal organization; fairly ruthless; will hire skilled ninja assassins and superpowered manhunters to track down and kill you

Disadvantages: Frequently slowed by his own organization's bloated and inefficient bureaucracy; rarely has superpowers of his own; often toppled by greed or congestive heart failure; definitely evil but deep down just an advanced version of the Masked Loser

Often heard saying: "Foolish insect! You have meddled in my affairs for the *last* time! I promise you, you will not *survive* our next meeting!"

Dr. Punching Bag
Also known as: the Screamer, Old Reliable, the Throbbing Vein, Professor Needy, Nice Try, Creepy

Advantages: Very ambitious; uses genius IQ or superpowers to either rule or destroy world (sometimes hedges bets and goes for both); will devise intricate plots and devices for the express purpose of killing you; attentive, meticulous, and utterly sociopathic; won't hesitate to murder innocent people; capable of forming deeply psychotic attachment to you that persists until killed or lobotomized

Disadvantages: Gets old after a while

Often heard saying: "I confess I expected more from the great [YOUR NAME HERE]. But no matter! Now that my android guards have sealed you inside my *brain-humidifier,* allow me to *explain* how I plan to *destroy the world!!*"

WHAT'S YOUR ARCHENEMY IQ?

Of course, knowing what kinds of supervillains are out there doesn't necessarily mean you'll intuitively sense which one will make for an ideal nemesis. For help in that area, you can turn to the Archenemy IQ Test™—just answer each question as honestly as you can and in no time at all you'll find yourself locked in mortal combat with a sinister and merciless foe!

1. Say you're on patrol in an unfamiliar city—where would you go if you wanted to encounter some satisfyingly deranged malcontent about to embark on a chillingly fiendish plot?
    a) The docks
    b) An abandoned factory
    c) A secret underwater base
    d) Evil seems to have a way of finding *you*
2. Which of these pick-up lines is most likely to work on you?
    a) "Roses are red, violets are blue, in exactly fifteen minutes I plan to unleash a plague of robotic leeches upon the city . . . unless you can stop me first."

b) "Do you know what would look good on you? An expression of absolute terror."

c) "Tell you what: I'll give you a thirty-second head start before unleashing my ravenous doom-hounds."

d) "Here's a quarter. Go call your next of kin."

3. You've managed to corner a brutal criminal. Since you know he won't allow himself to be taken alive, you hope he:

a) Launches one of his trademark deca-bombs at a supporting column, attempting to crush you both beneath a lethal deluge of stone and steel

b) Tosses a nullifier-grenade into an adjacent orphanage, making you choose between taking him down and saving the lives of hundreds of innocents

c) Grabs a young child or pregnant woman to use as a human shield

d) All of the above

4. Something has activated your crime-sensor. You bring up the satellite malfeasance system and see that your archnemesis has:

a) Miniaturized the city in hopes of creating a one-of-a-kind snow globe

b) Introduced a new line of evil toys featuring exposed metal edges, choking hazards, and anthrax-flavored plush

c) Started teaching evolution again

d) Opened an evil carnival filled with man-eating rides, bloodthirsty clowns, and flavorless sno-cones

5. Your archenemy has somehow managed to capture you. You hope he doesn't:

a) Strap you inside a giant piano and start playing "Chop-sticks"

b) Lash you to a conveyer belt that leads to an enormous hero-shredding machine

c) Lower you into a pit where you'll face your brainwashed comrade, teammate, or lover in brutal hand-to-hand combat

d) Discuss his religious beliefs

6. The event that led your archenemy to turn to a life of crime was:

a) The death or protracted illness of his beloved wife

b) The prejudice and hatred of those around him

c) Lack of other employment opportunities combined with a slow economy

d) Alien value system; i.e., knows nothing of our human concepts of "morality" or "take a penny, leave a penny"

7. After escaping from a maximum-security prison or insane asylum, your ideal archenemy would seek to avenge his imprisonment by:

a) Kidnapping your sidekick

b) Infiltrating and destroying your secret headquarters

c) Discovering your true identity and attacking your loved ones

d) Becoming a productive member of society

8. Your ideal supervillain knows that the best way to get your attention is by:

a) Slipping into the annual Philanthropist's Ball and then holding the city's wealthiest citizens hostage

b) Hijacking a nuclear missile

c) Imprisoning you in an alternate universe where meta-criminals are seen as authority figures

d) Casually running a hand through his hair and then fixing you with a sultry gaze

EVALUATING YOUR SCORE

To calculate your score, first assign each of your answers a numerical equivalent:

a) = 1; b) = 2; c) = 3; d) = 4

Now, add up your score and find your ideal archenemy type, using the key below:

32–24: You like 'em big and evil. Any supervillain that wants to catch your attention better power up his mass-decay accelerator, 'cause you're not leaving your headquarters for anything less.

23–16: You're interested in more than just the size of his evil plan. If a supervillain can prove to you that he's truly psychotic, you'll give him a chance.

15–8: You're just looking for a good time. Omniscient mega-villains, art smugglers, dope fiends—you'll pummel anyone.

HOW TO MEET SUPERVILLAINS

Instead of sitting around your secret headquarters, watching yet another superhero makeover on *You Go, Dyna-Girl!* and whining about how hard it is to meet people these days, it's time for you to take some action. After all, you're a superhero! Taking action is what you do best. Stop thinking of yourself as a lonely mega-loser and start thinking of yourself as a strong, independent hero who's in control of his or her own destiny—a destiny that will have you paired off with a vile supervillain by the time the next New Year's Eve rolls around.

Of course, it can be hard to get out there and meet new enemies, particularly when you don't even know where "out there" is. So here are some hints on where you can go to jump-start your search (as well as some places to avoid at all costs)!

Check out:

Crime Scenes and Disaster Areas
Supervillains are attracted to pain and suffering, so set your portable evil-detector to "misery," throw on a fresh cape, and scope out the scene at a nearby tragedy. You'd be surprised by how many evil geniuses you might find rubbernecking at a simple ethnic cleansing!

Adult Education Classes
There's nothing as sexy as a supervillain who's into self-improvement, so run, fly, or teleport on over to your local community college and pick up a course catalog. Remember, though, that you're here to meet your future archnemesis, not to make nice with fellow heroes—so look for classes like Ad-

vanced Plotting and Scheming, Introduction to Nihilism, and Public Threatening 101.

HELPFUL HINT ALERT!
Believe it or not, another great way to meet supervillains is by frequenting pet stores. That's right! But not because even the minions of darkness can't resist adorable puppies or fluffy kittens— they're there to buy food for their pet raptors, pythons, and man-eating plants. Believe me, you'd be surprised how quickly you can go through a box of Vulture Chow!

Religious Groups

Before you throw this book across the room in disgust, remember, people worship all sorts of things. Am I advocating that you waste your time with Promise Keepers or Jews for Jesus or some other notoriously pious organization? Of course not. But there are plenty of thriving religious denominations that attend to the spiritual ill-being of the supervillain community. So sit in on a black mass, join a local group as they sacrifice a virgin to Kali the Destroyer, or participate in a Necronomicon reading—that crafty gal beside you in the unholy circle might be exactly who you've been waiting for!

Gyms

Joining a gym is not only a good way to continue honing your powers, but it will also expose you to supervillains equally dedicated to fine-tuning theirs (though presumably for more ignoble purposes). These self-motivated evil-doers are exactly the type that you're looking to meet, and the gym environment helps smooth the always-awkward introduction. (For instance, even though "Can I spot you on that bus?" may not win any awards for cleverness, it beats "Say, didn't you try to take over the world a few years ago? Whatever happened with that?")

Meanwhile, avoid at all costs:

Bars and Nightclubs

What kind of supervillain wastes his or her evenings drinking or dancing instead of plotting to encase the city in a giant Jell-O mold? (Remember, most nightspots operate between 9 p.m. and 4 a.m., the same dark hours when evil plans are most likely to succeed.) And while it's true that you can sometimes find low-level criminals in certain waterfront bars, these blackguards should only be used for interrogation—no matter how nasty, venal, and satisfyingly grotesque they may appear, they are *not* to be considered archenemy material!

Volunteer Organizations and Charity Events

While there *are* so-called malevolent charities that attempt to raise money or provide services to headquarters-less or otherwise down-on-their-bad-luck supervillains, the best of these organizations are really just scams or fronts for money-laundering syndicates, while the worst of them actually appear to believe in "doing bad by doing good." Any supervillain you might meet at one of these functions is either an idiot or a con artist. Either way, I know you can do better.

Finding Your Nemesis Online

A particularly easy—and satisfyingly high-tech—way to get yourself out there is through an online personals service. As with everything, however, there is a right way and a wrong way to construct an online profile—and anyone who tells you otherwise probably spends their Friday nights watching *Doctor Who.* Here's what I'm talking about:

A TALE OF TWO PROFILES

Of the following two profiles, the first one (Exhibit A) is catchy and creative, while the second (Exhibit B) doesn't quite make the cut. And because both are *actual* profiles that I found while doing research for this chapter (of course, I changed all potentially identifying info), that means that somewhere out there is one very lonely superhero (and yes, I mean you, Janet348!).

User Name (Exhibit A)

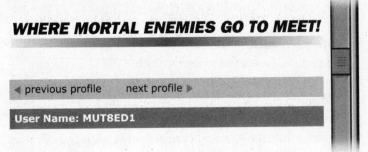

WHERE MORTAL ENEMIES GO TO MEET!

◄ previous profile   next profile ►

User Name: MUT8ED1

Why this works:

First of all, it's playful, punchy, and yes, even a little flirty. It alludes to this hero's power class (Transmutation) but it doesn't give too much away, leaving the supervillain curious about what other surprises this hero might have in store . . .

User Name (Exhibit B)

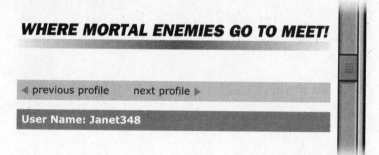

WHERE MORTAL ENEMIES GO TO MEET!

◄ previous profile   next profile ►

User Name: Janet348

Why this doesn't work:
I want to give this hero the benefit of the doubt, but looking at her user name, I first want to ask her: Hello? What are you thinking? The whole point of having a secret identity is that it's a secret. I mean, am I supposed to give you points for not using your last name?

Opening Line (Exhibit A)

Experienced superhero seeks villain to share companionship, brawling, brain-rattling punches.

Why this works:
Wow, what supervillain wouldn't be intrigued by that? Not only does this hero let us know exactly what she's looking for (no Mr. Small-Time for her!), but she manages to do so in a slightly self-

deprecating way that comes across as fresh and funny instead of chillingly pathetic.

Opening Line (Exhibit B)

Does she or doesn't she?

Why this doesn't work:
To be honest, this is not horrible. By managing to portray herself here as a tad arch and provocative, Janet348 has probably gotten some people to take a second look (assuming they'd gotten past the unfortunate name). But she still has a long way to go: she's now blown *two* chances to tell prospective archenemies either A) what she's looking for in a supervillain or B) what her superpowers are.

Song or Album That Puts Me in the Mood (Exhibit A)

I usually listen to Flight of the Valkyries before I
go out on patrol. Or We Will Rock You.
I'm not picky.

Why this works:
What can I say? With every opportunity, MUT8ED1 manages to make herself seem more and more interesting—both as a

person *and* a superhero. I may have to become a supervillain just so I can meet her!

Song or Album That Puts Me in the Mood (Exhibit B)

The Fugees, Tony Bennett, Coldplay. Anything from The Muppet Movie.

Why this doesn't work:

It could be that she's just trying to be funny. I hope so, because otherwise I'm afraid that Janet348 just doesn't seem to understand that the person she's trying to appeal to here is *evil.* And while I agree that puppets can be creepy, even if there were a supervillain out there who secretly could relate to Miss Piggy, is that really the sort of perverted slime that you'd want as your archenemy?

Celebrity I Resemble Most (Exhibit A)

I usually get Ultra-Lass, but without the mask. Or the whole 'I extrude exosenic acid through my pores' thing.

Why this works:

She's not setting up any unreasonable expectations here, but at the same time, hey, what supervillain wouldn't jump at the chance to do battle with a superhero who even *vaguely* resembles Ultra-Lass?

Celebrity I Resemble Most (Exhibit B)

I've been told Sarah Jessica Parker and Christina Aguilera. And once, some guy said Madonna, but that was during my pointy, cone-shaped bra period.

Why this doesn't work:

Not *celebrity*-celebrity! *Superhero*-celebrity! No supervillain's going to want to be seen locked in mortal combat with a skank like Christina! Remember who you're trying to appeal to here, people!

If I Could Be Anywhere at the Moment (Exhibit A)

In an alternate universe, facing incredible odds as part of a last-ditch battle that will decide the fate of our planet.

Why this works:

Ding-ding-ding! We have a winner! No pushing, boys.

If I Could Be Anywhere at the Moment (Exhibit B)

Cabo. Or Rio. Um, actually, it's a toss-up. Better just take me to both of them.

Why this doesn't work:
I wonder, has this person ever even *seen* a supervillain?

The Five Items I Can't Live Without (Exhibit A)

That's easy. Utility belt, length of silken cord, personal nullifier field, vibranium knife, and Ben & Jerry's Chunky Monkey. In that order.

Why this works:
Again, a delightful mix of punchy humor and important information. Supervillains who appreciate a resourceful adversary will nod approvingly upon reading this entry, as utility belts are typically the sign of a hero who strives to be prepared for anything and everything.

The Five Items I Can't Live Without (Exhibit B)

Cell phone, passport, books, love, deodorant.

Why this doesn't work:
Is it just me, or do *none* of those things have anything to do with crimefighting? Or superpowers? Or just, you know, kicking some degenerate ass?

More About What I'm Looking For (Exhibit A)

> Be cruelly vengeful, but not petty or spiteful. Be vicious, bold and sadistic, but not redundant or, even worse, boring. Stop talking about trapping me in some insanely intricate killing machine and just do it already! Basically, I've got a lot to offer and I'm looking for an archenemy who's ready to commit to a long-term relationship involving frequent brawling, a few doomsday machines, and lots of collateral damage. And yes, looks are important, but not as important as antisocial behavior or homicidal tendencies.

Why this works:

Again, this is specific without being dull. MUT8ED1 allows her sparkling personality to shine through while also being very straightforward about the qualities that are important to her in an archenemy. Trust me, this one won't be on the market for very long!

More About What I'm Looking For (Exhibit B)

> Someone who wants the world and isn't afraid to go after it. Someone who won't shy away from commitment and who will stick with the relationship even if things get rough sometimes (okay, so maybe I'm a little challenging—I'm worth it!). Someone who bathes regularly and can make me laugh. Someone who maybe used Drakkar Noir in high school, but hasn't touched the stuff in years. Bonus points if you're a firestarter or risk-taker!

Why this doesn't work:

This is another one of those entries that fills me with hope initially, only to leave me utterly disappointed. For the first time I felt that Janet348 was really "speaking" to the brainsick scientists and undead sorcerers who would be reading her profile. Clearly, she wants to be with an ambitious evil-doer with world domination on his mind. But then she backs away from this with frivolous qualifications like "bathing." The final mention that she's looking for a supervillain with fire-related powers does offer a glimmer of hope, however.

LET'S MEET . . . L-235!

For years L-235 was thought to be "just another asteroid," but "that was only part of its devilishly clever charade." In fact, this "crafty foe" was "just pretending to hurtle aimlessly through space" while all along "headed for a kamikaze tour of the Northern Hemisphere . . . or possibly the moon." "Even experienced heroes will be pleasantly surprised" by this adversary's "lack of humanity and cursedly dense iron-nickel core." While some claim that "it's just a hunk of inert rock," to others L-235 has proven itself "worthy of serious consideration as one of the great, all-time supervillains." (Note: L-235 is not a recommended adversary for novice superheroes.) —from *Mister Mental's Survey of Supervillains,* 2003 edition

NURTURING A NEW ARCHNEMESIS RELATIONSHIP

So let's say you're at an event, maybe a meta-human cocktail party arranged by a local superhero team, and you happen to spot a yummy-looking supervillain. How the heck are you supposed to get his attention, much less start thwarting his attempts at world domination? Thanks once again to my extensive work with both sides of this equation (supervillains and superheroes), I can offer vital answers and essential tips on this subject, beginning with these three simple rules:

Rule 1: *Don't seem too eager.* That's right: If the hotline starts flashing, take if off the hook. If your evil-detecting equipment lights up, throw an old cape over the console. If you happen to notice your insignia-alert splashed across the night sky, close the blast doors. Sure, you may be pacing through your secret headquarters waiting for your potential nemesis to commit some unspeakable act of destruction, but he or she doesn't have to know that. Play it cool. After all, you're in no rush—you've got *lots* of other evil-doers to thwart, right? (Wink, wink!)

Rule 2: *Act like you're doing them a favor.* No matter what brand of evil they're perpetrating, always make it seem like you've got better things to do. For instance:

- "You're holding the city hostage with a giant brain magnet? Uh-huh. And who is this again?"
- "Gee, you've just tainted the city's water supply with a mutagenic virus and the antidote is hidden in a secret

location? Hmm. You know, ordinarily, I'd love to help out, it's just, well, it's kind of last minute and I was planning on foiling something else tonight."

Remember, you can't let them think you're prepared to drop everything and come running just because a few thousand people are in imminent danger of being identified by their dental records.

Rule 3: *Wait at least a day before confounding an insidious scheme, master plan, or doomsday plot.* Even if that hidden gamma bomb is on a timer, *you're* not. Make sure that this supervillain is right for you before committing to thwart some elaborate plan (such as a conspiracy to hijack the Vatican). Insist on starting off with more casual acts of evil, such as civil disobedience or swapping music online.

HEALING THE ARCHNEMESIS RELATIONSHIP

The Patrioteer and *Hell-Droid* had been archenemies for more than seven years when they first came to see me. While they both agreed that in the beginning they had despised each other almost immediately—the Patrioteer described it as "an almost magical loathing"—as the years went by they noticed that a creeping sense of empathy and compassion had begun to undermine their mutual hatred.

Longing to rekindle those early feelings of antipathy and loathing, but increasingly frustrated by their growing affection for one another, they had just about decided to give up when another couple suggested they attend one of my weekend retreats. They agreed to give it a shot, but without much hope of success. "We've tried everything to make this relationship work," explained Hell-Droid. "But it's no use. I used to obsess about different ways to destroy him, and now? The other day I actually caught myself wondering if he was getting enough to eat."

During the next few days, the Patrioteer and Hell-Droid not only learned that what they were experiencing was normal, they discovered that there were things they could do to revitalize their once-strong bond of disgust and bitter hostility. You see, too often we forget that, as well as a desperate struggle for survival, archenemies are involved in a *relationship*.

Of course, relationships need constant nurturing in order to thrive. Ignoring our archenemy relationships results in a gradual loss of hostility and enmity. In some cases, prolonged neglect will even accelerate the appearance of dangerously sincere emotions such as fondness or understanding. Throughout the rest of this chapter, I'll offer techniques and tips that will help you turn every encounter with your nemesis into an opportunity to build *real* hatred and abhorrence.

Is Your Relationship on Life Support?

Is your relationship just experiencing a passing spasm of perfunctory courtesy? Or is it laid up with a full-blown case of tearful compassion? Take the following two-part quiz to find out if you and your significantly evil other are still fit to be called "archenemies":

PART 1

1. **My nemesis doesn't really listen when I tell him to "Drop that electro-rifle" or "Put down those Rygellian nullifier crystals."**

   ☐ Strongly disagree   ☐ Somewhat disagree   ☐ No opinion
   ☐ Somewhat agree   ☐ Strongly agree

2. **When I'm with my archenemy, I often fantasize about battling other supervillains.**

   ☐ Strongly disagree   ☐ Somewhat disagree   ☐ No opinion
   ☐ Somewhat agree   ☐ Strongly agree

3. **My teammates think of my nemesis and I as bitter enemies.**

   ☐ Strongly disagree   ☐ Somewhat disagree   ☐ No opinion
   ☐ Somewhat agree   ☐ Strongly agree

4. **My archenemy completely satisfies my need for fierce, no-holds-barred conflict.**

   ☐ Strongly disagree   ☐ Somewhat disagree   ☐ No opinion
   ☐ Somewhat agree   ☐ Strongly agree

5. **I feel that my archenemy's schemes are just as diabolical and insidious now as when we first started fighting.**

   ☐ Strongly disagree   ☐ Somewhat disagree   ☐ No opinion
   ☐ Somewhat agree   ☐ Strongly agree

EVALUATING YOUR SCORE

To calculate your score, assign each of your answers a numerical equivalent. At the end of the quiz, you'll add your score from Part 1 to your score from Part 2 to find your evil-doing potential.

**Strongly agree = 5; Somewhat agree = 4; No opinion = 3
Somewhat disagree = 2; Strongly disagree = 1**

PART 2

6. Now let's try some word association—which sets of words spring to mind when thinking of your relationship with your archenemy?
   a) Hostile, deadly, crafty
   b) Indifferent, depressed, semiretired
   c) Psychotic, vicious, genocidal
   d) Warm, gracious, fuzzy

7. How do you and your archenemy resolve arguments or disagreements?
   a) Savage combat
   b) Heated discussion
   c) High-energy plasma blasts
   d) Hug-a-thon

8. What quality do you like best about your archenemy?
   a) His insatiable bloodlust
   b) Her violent temper
   c) The voices in his head
   d) His rock-hard abs

9. How did the two of you recently commemorate your first meeting?

a) Returned to top-secret laboratory to try and recapture some of that old animosity
b) A killing spree, accompanied by a series of elaborately grotesque clues
c) A dramatic rooftop battle
d) Cuddling

EVALUATING YOUR SCORE

To calculate your score, first assign each of your answers a numerical equivalent:

a) = 1; b) = 2; c) = 3; d) = 4

Now, add up your scores from both parts of the quiz to find out whether your relationship is:

36–29: Dangerously harmonious
28–19: Uncomfortably cozy
18–9: Lethal

The wrong way to meet supervillains.

HOW TO COMMUNICATE HATEFUL EMOTIONS

If you suddenly find yourself trapped in a caring, supportive relationship, the first person to look to is yourself. Only by taking full responsibility for your role in creating this situation can you begin to change it. Since the foundation of all satisfyingly abusive relationships is cruelly honest communication, it should come as no surprise to discover that the most dysfunction and compassion is related to poor communication skills. Only when you seek to use words to invalidate your partner's feelings, judge his or her actions unfairly, and belittle, blame, hurt, and criticize, are you being an effective communicator. Examine the following chart and see if any of these communication pitfalls sound familiar.

You say:	But your archenemy hears:	So instead try:
"You killed Mega-Hound! You monster! Why would you do such a thing? Why?! Just tell me why!!!"	"I am interested in the motives behind your actions. Please tell me more about your reasons for killing my animal sidekick. I care about you and am interested in you!"	"It hurts me that you disintegrated my faithful sidekick. Mega-Hound didn't deserve to die that way. Fear my retribution."
"You think that energy blast is going to stop me? When a liberal application of Oint-	"I understand that you're confused about why your energy blast didn't kill me. I hope	"I'm disappointed that you thought I would be that easy to destroy, particularly

ment X will transform me into Cellulo, Amazing Master of Permeability?"	that by explaining my superpower to you I can help you launch more effective attacks in the future."	when I have super powers of my own. Discover foryourself the wispy and in substantial nature of my wrath."
"No, don't touch that! You don't know what you're doing! You fool, that's the release mechanism for the Vorland chamber— you'll kill us all!!"	"Please, I care about you and I don't want you to come to any harm. You're important to me."	"I disagree with your decision to unseal the Vorland chamber, but I respect your suicidal urges. However, please wait until my comrades and I can escape in our rocket-pod before proceeding with your thoroughly self-destructive plans."

Using Written Communications to Build Abhorrence

I personally find it difficult, if I happen to feel contented or satisfied for some reason, to summon up the negative emotions that are so essential to maintaining a healthy archenemy relationship. In order to compensate for that weakness, I developed the technique of writing a hate letter to one's nemesis. The simple act of writing such a letter, even if you never send it, is sure to inflame your smoldering fury. Many a time I've begun writing a letter in a state of mild irritation only to find that by the

time I'm through I've become seized by a delightfully incoher-
ent rage. Read on for tips on composing an effective hate letter
as well as a sample you can use to help get started.

> Dear Iron Pharaoh,
> It hurts me when you try to use your tractor beam to shift the Moon's
> orbit and swamp North America. It makes me angry that every time I
> spare your life, you just turn around and infect me with an alien para-
> site. I wish you could see how you disappoint me when you turn your
> earthquake ray on downtown Apex City. I am sad that deep down you're
> nothing but a homicidal maniac. I'm embarrassed that I seem unable to
> kill you—the world would be a better place without you. And I can't be-
> lieve you thought anyone would believe that evil clone was really me.
> Finally, yes, I am still furious that you tried to brainwash my own side-
> kick and have him kill me.
> Yours truly,
> Doctor Metropolis
>
> P.S. You suck.

If you're having trouble getting started, here are a few lead-in
phrases that you can use to get the bile flowing:

- "I want to kill you when . . ."
- "You will understand the true meaning of pain once I . . ."
- "I feel annoyed that you tried to destroy . . ."
- "I hope it hurts real bad when I   "
- "I feel embarrassed that I couldn't stop you from . . ."

- "I hope the next time you get caught in a dimensional vortex you . . ."
- "Say 'hi' to . . ."
- "The weather here is . . ."

THE END OF THE INNOCENCE

"In 1970, soon after the creation of the BMHA, Congress slashed the Manhattan Project's funding, and by the end of the year, what was left of the Project had been absorbed by the BMHA and 'repurposed' as its research arm. But did the end of the Manhattan Project mean that the government had lost its interest in superheroes? Or was it simply a change in tactics? A small cubicle in the White House basement held the answer. There, the special advisor to the president on meta-human affairs, the beautiful Dr. Victoria Vanguard, was hard at work on the Ford administration's new meta-human threat assessment report.

"According to Dr. Vanguard's theories, meta-human development couldn't be sustained outside its natural evolutionary track, but such development could be enhanced indirectly. In other words, if you wanted to continue to promote the sustainable evolution of superheroes, you couldn't do it in a laboratory, but you could do certain things environmentally to accelerate the natural process. And with whispered reports circulating of something called a 'hero gap' between the United States and the Soviet Union, this was good news indeed.

"The hero gap meant the administration couldn't be expected to wait around for people to stumble across strangely glowing meteorites or be granted awesome new powers by dying aliens. So, adopting Dr. Vanguard's prescriptions, the government began producing a torrent of legislation designed to encourage the development of meta-powers in human populations. Specifically, this meant rolling back certain well intentioned but naive environmental protection laws that were unfairly restricting people's access to toxic chemicals, radioactive isotopes, experimental drugs, and top-secret weapons. It also meant encouraging industry to become more involved in the sloppy transportation and storage of such substances. Meanwhile, warnings that this wave of corporate welfare would lead to what some termed 'a super-hero-industrial complex,' whose concerns would come to dominate domestic and foreign policy, were studiously ignored."

    —from *God Among the Ruins: How Congress and American Business Created a New Master Race,* by S. James-Smyth

Chapter Thirteen

Justice Leagues, Job Hunts, and the Superheroic Résumé

For most of our profession's history, particularly during the early years, becoming a superhero was a fairly straightforward process. With no regulatory oversight or state licensing agencies, the process of actually achieving superhero status rarely involved more than donning a costume, adopting a persona, and lashing out at the forces of villainy and chaos.

In today's globalized economy, however, not only are superheroes required to obtain a license, but they also must contend with downsizing, cheap immigrant superheroes, and even meta-human outsourcing. Meanwhile, as the ranks of domestic heroes have continued to swell, the number of available supervillains has remained steady at best, meaning that each hero must work harder to battle the same amount of evil he was fighting just a few years ago. (The only good news in all this is that supervillains don't have it any easier—just check out the price tags on the latest weather-control machines if you don't believe me.)

I'm not telling you all this to depress you; yes, the superhero market is far more competitive today than it has been at any other point in our history, but there are still plenty of crimefighting opportunities out there, if you know how to look for them. So before you even think about prowling dangerous back alleys or brooding impressively from the top of gargoyle-encrusted buildings, promise me you'll do two things:

1. Read this chapter.
2. And then read it again.

Why? Because this chapter will teach you how to:

- Apply for a superpower operating license
- Join your local professional superhero association
- Identify your personality type and discover what working environment best suits you
- Secure a position with a crusading duo, superheroic team, or mighty legion

---

HELPFUL HINT ALERT!

You may soon hit a point where you're facing more evil than you can handle by yourself, but not enough to warrant joining or forming a super-organization of some sort. When that happens, you may want to consider recruiting a sidekick. In addition to running errands and providing much-needed homoerotic tension, sidekicks make incredibly good hostages (be mindful of certain child-labor laws, however, which restrict the number of hours an underage sidekick can serve as a decoy or bait). The following are some good questions to ask when interviewing candidates:

- "Why do you want to be a sidekick?"
- "Can you tell me about a time when you were captured and then imprisoned in a giant blender?"
- "If you could have any superpower other than the one you already have, what would it be and why?"
- "Tell me why I should hire you instead of some space monkey."
- "What do you feel is your greatest weakness?" (Note: Make sure that you and your sidekick don't *both* have a fatal sensitivity to, for example, red electricity or argonite.)

THE VALUE OF A PROFESSIONAL ASSOCIATION

Ask any hero, "What's the greatest challenge you've faced in your career?" and the answer may surprise you. More often than not, instead of the *Enigma Paradox* or the *Phantom Wars*, you're likely to hear about the many obstacles they faced when just starting out. Of course, you might already know what they're talking about. And with everything you've got on your plate—from trying to maintain a secret identity to shopping for a secret headquarters—joining a professional superhero association probably feels like the last thing you have time for.

However, the benefits of joining such an association are the very things that will make this transitional period that much

LET'S MEET . . . THE STEEL TURBAN!

Though this renegade magician "may be a little too flamboyant for some tastes," he still "delivers a pleasingly diabolical experience" once you "get past the ruffled shirt." "Driven by an insatiable lust for hair-care products and leather pants," the Steel Turban "escaped from a maximum-security dinner theater facility in the late '80s" and "promptly embarked on a wild, violent spree" of "ritualistic killings" and "fabulous TV specials." While the *Weird Warrior*, aka Taboo Ra, claims to have killed him, "no body was ever found"—"unless you count the rogue sorcerer's singed pelt of chest hair"—and some heroes believe that "the Turban is still alive," possibly "hiding out in Vegas," or "more likely, the Catskills," "injecting himself with massive doses of Propecia" and "plotting his revenge."   —from *Mister Mental's Survey of Supervillains,* 2003 edition

less stressful. For example, a well known, respected organization such as the International Brotherhood of Super-heroes not only offers a wide variety of workshops and seminars to help you get started, but also sponsors networking functions and career fairs. To help you learn more about the valuable role that professional organizations play in the superheroic community, I've included some excerpts from the IBSH Web site. If what you see here intrigues you, go to *www.ibsh.org* to learn more (see *Figure 2-2*).

GETTING YOUR OPERATING LICENSE

One area in which you'll find that the resources of the IBSH really come in handy is in taking the Superpower Operator

http://www.ibsh.org

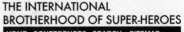

THE INTERNATIONAL BROTHERHOOD OF SUPER-HEROES

HOME CONFERENCES SEARCH SITEMAP

Our Mission

For more than 100 years, the International Brotherhood of Super-Heroes has supported the costumed crimefighting industry through public awareness campaigns, professional development opportunities, and career placement assistance.

What IBSH Does For You

We serve our members in several ways, including:

- Urging countries around the world to support pro-superhero policies, such as easy financing for tall, grappling-hook-friendly buildings; subsidized genetic tampering; and the ready availability of street-legal ray-guns and atomic morphifiers
- Ensuring a strong domestic superhero presence through better enforcement of existing immigration laws and the introduction of new trade regulations aimed at curbing meta-human outsourcing
- Capitalizing on the untapped forces of evil currently languishing in our penal system by promoting the use of human subjects in the (mostly unnecessary) testing of chemical and industrial by-products

IBSH Conferences, Publications, and Awards

Three more ways that IBSH helps our members meet their professional goals are through our peer-reviewed flagship publication, The IBSH-Signal; our twice-yearly symposium and industry convention (Calling all heroes! The next one is being held in sunny Boca Raton, Florida!); and finally, our professional awards, such as the Recognition for Best Use of Alien Power Device, which offer our members the chance to be recognized by their peers for their various outstanding achievements over the past year.

Figure 2-2

License (or SOL) exam. It's no secret that, even when used with the best of intentions, instruments such as guns, cars, or even drum machines can be deadly if wielded by the unskilled or very upset. Superpowers are no different. Therefore, the three-tiered SOL rating system was developed in order to help regulate their use and promote their responsible deployment.

CLASS A: Is permitted to battle any supervillain whose declared goal is personal vengeance, the accumulation of material wealth, or localized (no more than five city blocks) mayhem.

CLASS B: Is permitted to battle any Class A supervillain *as well as* any villain who pursues world domination, mass murder, or apocalypse. While these supervillains should demonstrate viable superpowers, Class B heroes may also challenge those villains who exhibit no abilities beyond a sort of unusual organizational capacity or singular perspicacity.

CLASS C: Is permitted to battle any Class A or B supervillain *as well as* any supervillain who threatens the existence of our solar system, galaxy, dimension, or space-time continuum (i.e., "reality as we know it").

Only those who can pass the three-part superpower operator exam will go on to receive their license. The exam itself is broken down as follows: Part 1 is a 100-question, multiple-choice test; Part 2 is an oral examination administered by three SHLA-qualified BMHA facilitators; and Part 3 consists of various field trials appropriate to your particular power class. The following sample questions are from Part 1 of the SOL exam.* Answers to

---

* These questions will not necessarily appear on the examination.

all of the sample questions can be found online at the IBSH
Web site. Good luck!

1. When a supervillain persists in trying to engage you in con-
   versation while fighting, you should:
   a) Keep quiet and hope he makes a fatal error
   b) Ask him if he'd rather go someplace quiet where the two
      of you can chat
   c) Slip in a few probing questions about the exact nature of
      his nefarious scheme
   d) Slap him in the mouth with a witty riposte and a Chevy
      Blazer

2. When the woman you love, who is secretly a supervillain
   but still possesses several admirable qualities, is killed by her
   former master, you should:
   a) Brood inconsolably in your headquarters
   b) Brood inconsolably in your command center
   c) Brood inconsolably from the tops of gothic cathedrals or
      skyscrapers
   d) Go insane

3. When sacrificing yourself to save the lives of billions of innocent people, you should:
   a) Caress the cheek of your teammate/lover and say some-
      thing lighthearted and brave, like "Don't miss me too
      much, okay?"
   b) Caress the cheek of your teammate/lover and say some-
      thing noble and inspiring, like "I love you but . . . I have
      to do this. I hope that someday you'll understand."
   c) Caress the cheek of your teammate/lover and say some-

thing tragic and mournful, like "A part of me will always be with you. Farewell, my love."

d) Caress the cheek of your teammate/lover and thoughtlessly blurt out, "I did it with Man-Tank while you were trapped in the Infinity Zone. But it didn't mean anything, I swear."

4. The proper terminology to use when describing the strange phenomenon that has transported you to an alternate world where the Nazis won World War II is:

a) "It must be some kind of *cosmic disturbance!*"

b) "It must be some kind of *rift in the space-time continuum!*"

c) "It must be some kind of *localized dimensional anomaly!*"

d) All of the above

5. When being crushed to death by a powerful supervillain, you should use your last ounce of strength to:

a) Contribute to the sum total of human knowledge by offering a detailed description of the physical sensation of dying, i.e., "Can't breathe . . . losing consciousness . . ."

b) Fling one final, defiant curse at your adversary, i.e., "Enjoy it while it lasts, you monster, because you won't look half this good after I'm through with you!"

c) Strain to reach the hidden switch on your utility belt that activates your miniature anti-crushing device

d) Weep bitterly

6. When your teammate, whom everyone was certain had been killed when Lord Havok's secret island headquarters exploded, is revealed to be alive, your first reaction should be:

a) "Thank god you're alive! But . . . *how?*"

b) "I . . . I saw you when the island's anti-matter generator exploded. I saw you *die* . . ."

c) "Hmm. No one could have survived an explosion of that magnitude. So who are you, I wonder? An evil clone sent by Lord Havok to deceive us? Or perhaps some kind of . . . shapeshifter?"

d) "You're back! What did you bring me?"

7. Whenever your partner or teammate falls under the mental control of a powerful supervillain, you should try to get them to snap out of it by:

   a) Gently reminding them of the bond you share (and, if appropriate, of those "special moments" together in the danger room after the last holiday party)

   b) Shaking them violently, then slapping them around a little

   c) Tenderly reformatting their brain

   d) Ignoring them and hoping they come to their senses

8. When a godlike being transports you to a distant world and forces you to participate in some brutal gladiatorial contest, you should:

   a) Refuse to participate, arguing that the essence of humanity lies in its ability to value all life equally

   b) Compete in the arena, but defy your captor by showing mercy to your vanquished opponents

   c) Spread the ideals of freedom and self-determination among your fellow combatants and lead a revolt

   d) Show these off-world turkeys how it's done and totally kick some alien ass

9. This sign indicates which of the following:

a) Hurricane shelter
b) Weather powers permitted next one hundred feet
c) Caution, waterspouts
d) Time warp ahead

10. This sign indicates which of the following:

a) Caution, giant Rollo ahead
b) To access tunnel, tear along dotted line
b) Hidden entrance to secret headquarters, next right
c) None of the above

DEFINING YOUR SUPERHEROIC PERSONALITY: MAKING USE OF THE MSTI

In our society, when a hero passes his licensing exam and receives his operator rating, it's treated as a graduation of sorts. Parties are thrown, toasts are made, and family members eagerly press the new superhero about his career plans (provided, of course, that you're not a Crimefighter hero whose family has been recently slaughtered). They ask: Will you be spending a few years sidekicking for an established hero? Are you going to try and join one of the big justice leagues? Or are you planning on going out on your own? As for the hero, he's often so eager to begin challenging the forces of evil that he naively jumps at the first opportunity to come his way.

But accepting a position out of enthusiasm or desperation and then hoping for the best is no way to embark on a career. Studies have shown that when a hero selects a crimefighting environment that complements his specific *interdictive personality*,

---

HELPFUL HINT ALERT!

If you have difficulty relating to others and don't mind a sidekick who will occasionally feel the need to bury his nose in your crotch or sleep on the hood of your hover-car, then you may want to consider an animal sidekick. Flying canines, super-strong felines, and invulnerable goats all make excellent allies and great all-around companions. Here are a few tips to help ease the transition to working with a four-legged super-friend:

- Help them understand the crucial difference between a delivery man and a supervillain
- Their poopy may be highly toxic or radioactive, so be sure you're qualified to handle and remove it
- Always remember to praise them hysterically whenever they defeat a supervillain; also, reward them with a chew-toy or belly rub
- Don't call them by their alter-ego names while battling supervillains; if their archenemies were to discover that, for instance, Rex the Ultra-Hound is really Tipsy the Scottish terrier, you could be putting your sidekick in grave danger

he's more likely to feel successful and fulfilled. Unfortunately, most of us have spent our entire lives trying to be the kind of superhero that *others* want us to be—rarely do we feel like we have any say in the matter.

But now, with the help of the Martel-Spry Type Indicator (MSTI), you can discover and learn to embrace your authentic self. A system for uncovering and making sense of superheroic personality types, the MSTI cultivates a level of self-awareness that enables you to make appropriate and rewarding career choices. Which crimefighting situation—partnership, team, justice league, or legion—is right for you? Let the MSTI help you find the answer!

The four MSTI dimensions are listed as two pairs of opposites:

Pummeling (PM)/Outwitting (OT)

- Those who exhibit Pummeling traits tend to approach crimefighting in a direct, often spectacularly brutal manner
- Those who exhibit Outwitting traits tend to seek a more flexible, creative solution

Swashbuckling (SW)/Brooding (BR)

- Those who exhibit Swashbuckling traits get their energy from vivid, flamboyant displays of superheroic verve and panache
- Those who exhibit Brooding traits get their energy from suppressed rage and a complex web of interlocking neuroses and obscure psychosexual issues

Their poopy may be highly toxic.

Finding Your Type

The following twenty-four-statement inventory will help you un-cover your unique personality type. Read each statement care-fully and then indicate your response using the following system:

0 - not like me at all
1 - somewhat like me
2 - exactly like me

___ **1.** I feel awkward in sprawling, multidimensional con-flicts, but I enjoy battling one-on-one with someone I feel connected to.

___ **2.** I get energized when stalking my quarry from the shad-ows.

___ **3.** I enjoy being the focus of a particle destabilizer.

___ **4.** I am comfortable challenging and battling new villains.

___ **5.** I always like to wait for my fellow heroes before charg-ing into the fray.

___ 6. I prefer to spend most of my free time alone with my increasingly grim and violent thoughts.

___ 7. I tend to have a few close archenemies rather than a lot of casual adversaries.

___ 8. People often perceive me as "ruthless" or "vengeful."

___ 9. I feel drained if I use my powers for several consecutive periods without allowing myself some time to rest and recharge.

___ 10. I'm more likely to try and hurl a dimensional-compression bomb into outer space than attempt to defuse it.

___ 11. If I'm forced to choose between throwing a bus at a supervillain and immobilizing him by smashing open a water main and then using my ice-breath to encase him in a block of ice, I will throw the bus.

___ 12. I rely on hunches, magickal divination, and the confessions I can beat out of low-level criminals for a lot of my information.

___ 13. I find it hard to relax or concentrate if my secret headquarters is under attack by a giant robot.

___ 14. I often wait until the last minute before decisively vanquishing a supervillain or other threat to humanity.

___ 15. I value my ability to make pithy, topical remarks even in the heat of battle.

___ 16. I prefer to let my ominous presence and intimidating appearance speak for me.

___ 17. It is important to me to defeat a supervillain or alien overlord in front of a large crowd, so that others can be inspired by my feats of heroism.

___ **18.** People tend to seek me out for protection against things like giant mutant insects or Atlantean overlords intent on conquering the surface world.

___ **19.** When I disagree with people, it is difficult for me to keep from vaporizing them with my heat vision.

___ **20.** I value my ability to punch through solid steel.

___ **21.** People sometimes see me as little better than the psychopathic scum I track down and savagely pulpify.

___ **21a.** Sometimes I see myself as little better than the psychopathic scum I track down and savagely pulpify.

___ **22.** I spend considerable time trying to figure out how to return to my homeworld, Talus 9.

___ **23.** I make "to thwart" lists and feel satisfied when I can check off a thwarted supervillain.

___ **24.** I consider it more important to be invulnerable than to have X-ray vision.

Now it's time to add up your score. Once you've found your type, read on to learn more about how to use this information to find a working environment that will suit your temperament.

If you scored 18 or lower, you are a PMSW.
If you scored between 19 and 35, you are an OTSW.
If you scored between 36 and 53, you are a PMBR.
If you scored a 54 or higher, you are an OTBR.

PMSW—Pummeling Swashbuckling Type

Fearless, impulsive, and always willing to look on the bright side, PMSWs attack life with the same belligerent enthusiasm that they do supervillains. Their standard approach to any problem is to subject it to the mightiness of their superpowers. When faced with a multitude of options or tasks, PMSWs may take on too many projects at once, so supervisors should make a point of helping these heroes prioritize (e.g., subdue the evil mastermind *first*, and *then* focus on destroying his army of killer cyborgs). While PMSWs are often invulnerable, this power does not extend to their feelings: extremely sensitive, PMSWs may become discouraged by what they perceive as a rebuke or slight. Most comfortable in a team or league environment, it's essential that PMSWs feel they have the complete support of colleagues and managers in order to do their best work.

Suggestions for PMSW Types

- Surround yourself with people who respect the flailing, indiscriminate savagery of your approach. Remember, you don't need to justify yourself to anyone.
- Beware the temptation to use your powers simply to get attention. Learn to be more direct. It's OK to ask for what you need.
- Remember to stay focused—don't allow yourself to be distracted by lowly henchmen while your true quarry slips away in his escape pod.
- Talk to yourself in nurturing and caring ways. Don't wait for others to tell you that you're doing great—pat *yourself* on the back once in a while!

**LET'S MEET . . . THE UNDETERMINED
MINORITY SUPERVILLAIN!**

"An unexpectedly successful" result of the "groundbreaking 1972
Meta-human Civil Rights Amendment," the Undetermined
Minority Supervillain position is "a rotating slot that gives de-
serving minority criminal masterminds the opportunity to become a true discredit to their race." To qualify for "this highly
coveted position," candidates should be able to demonstrate "at
least three years of violently psychotic or antisocial behavior,"
"have a culturally consistent or ethnically topical persona and
costume" (i.e., *Negro-Man, Black Fist, Drunken Apache,* the
Yellow Devil), and also be "on the books as a member of an
oppressed minority group." But "ten-gallon supervillains should
beware": ever since "the landmark *Atomic-Hombre vs. the State of
Texas* ruling, Undetermined Minority Supervillain status is *not*
recognized by the Lone Star State. —from *Mister Mental's Survey
of Supervillains,* 2003 edition

OTSW—Outwitting Swashbuckling Type

Outgoing, resourceful, and supremely confident in their abilities, OTSWs work best when they're given the flexibility to use
their superpowers and management skills without regard for
private property or civilian populations. Highly motivated and
driven, they are usually the first ones in the secret headquarters
in the morning and the last to be retinally scanned at the end of
the day. When placed in leadership roles, OTSWs quickly rise
to the occasion, their clearly defined notions of duty and responsibility making it impossible for them to do anything less

than their best. Finally, though some OTSWs have been successful operating as solo heroes, their organizational talents and strong interpersonal skills make them much better suited to a team crimefighting situation.

Suggestions for OTSW Types
- In order to gain acceptance for your plans, use some sort of nifty holographic device for your group presentations. Remember, a solution rendered in 3-D is going to be that much more compelling.
- Resist the temptation to deal only with urgent, high-profile threats, like a Shi'ar battle group stationed in geosynchronous orbit over Washington, DC; don't forget to also wage war against illiteracy and childhood obesity.
- Avoid taking on so much at once that you feel scattered, frazzled, or overextended. If you find yourself facing *Mama*

HELPFUL HINT ALERT!

The following is a list of some stereotypical heroic actions and situations you'll want to try and avoid. Once considered career-builders, these have become so overused of late that they're now "cheesy." Though you may be forced to fall back on them in a pinch, keep their overall use to a minimum.

- Having a supervillain suffer amnesia or go insane immediately *after* discovering your secret identity (even worse: while insane, everyone dismisses this priceless information as the ravings of a madman!)

- Straining to pull a supervillain to safety as he dangles over a precipice or chasm (even worse: he slips out of his glove or his costume rips, and he falls anyway!)
- Chasing a shapely she-villain, cornering her, and then—after she boldly kisses you—being thrown you off your game and allowing her to escape
- Picking up a tank or other armored vehicle and shaking it until the soldiers or henchmen come tumbling out
- Getting hypnotized or brainwashed by a supervillain and being forced to commit crimes against your will (even worse: being hunted by other superheroes while trying to clear your name!)
- Rescuing sidekick or colleague even though you know it's a trap
- Tying villains up and leaving them for the police to take care of (even worse: wrapping a steel girder around them instead of simply using rope or twine!)

Voodoo, Razorstrike Jr., and the *Legion of Khaos* all at the same time, remember to delegate some of these confrontations to your colleagues; they'll probably be flattered to be asked, and more than happy to help out.

PMBR—Pummeling Brooding Type
Though PMBRs often come across as sullen, aloof, or feral, this is rarely an accurate reflection of their complex internal world. While PMBR types tends to cluster in the Transmutation Class, and thus often experience the feelings of persecution and alien-

ation that come from being hunted by government agents, this type is found in all power classes. Quiet, reserved, and introspective, PMBRs have difficulty communicating verbally and therefore often resort to extravagant displays of violence as their only means of expression. Though surprisingly intelligent, the fact that PMBRs typically possess devastating superpowers makes them more likely to adopt a head-on approach to problem-solving. This inflexible, somewhat impulsive approach, plus their general inability to maintain a tidy workspace, makes it difficult for PMBRs to function happily in a team environment.

Suggestions for PMBR Types

- Suppress the impulse to wreak mindless havoc. Strive to be mindful in whatever havoc you may wreak.
- Make time for artistic pursuits or hobbies. Gardening, bee-keeping, and bookbinding are wonderful ways to take a break from the stress and angst of being a super-strong freak with nickel-plated skin.
- Learn to say "no" sometimes. Believe it or not, you're probably *not* the only superhero in the world that can stop the Mole-People's invasion. Set some boundaries for yourself and others.

OTBR—Outwitting Brooding Type

Moody, irritable, and frequently psychotic, OTBRs experience an intense, often overwhelming need to punish evil-doers. Driven by some traumatic event from their past, such as the death of their parents or loved ones at the hands of a supervillain, OTBRs quickly develop a highly personal concept of justice that is refreshingly free of civil liberties or the rule of law. Intensely individualistic, OTBRs will nevertheless consent to a leadership role if a group's current leader has just been atomized. In general, though, this type is not suited to a group environment, as the gung-ho optimism of OTSW types tends to grate on the OTBRs' darker sensibilities. However, given the possibility that, if left to their own devices, the OTBR may descend irretrievably into a personal mythology of bloody retribution, it's often necessary to encourage OTBRs to maintain some affiliative links with a larger superhero organization, such as a justice league or legion.

Suggestions for OTBR Types

- Share your ideas, feelings, and violent fantasies only with those people that you feel close to.
- Try to be direct in your communications. Veiled threats or implied challenges may leave your adversaries feeling confused and unwanted.
- Be realistic about how others see you. Understand that rejection of your ruthless vigilante style is not necessarily a rejection of *you*.

"Don't get left behind! Tell your congressman,
'I want a nuclear waste dump in *my* backyard!'"
—from a 1964 Manhattan Project
public awareness campaign

APPLYING FOR A POSITION WITH A SUPERHEROIC ORGANIZATION

Now that you have some sense of the kind of the situation you're best suited for, whether it's operating as a solo crime-fighter, working with a partner, or as a member of a team, justice league, or legion, it's time to begin your job search. Personally, I'm still a fan of using the help-wanted ads found either online or in the classified section of your local newspaper. They can be a valuable and largely untapped source for leads, *if* you know what to look for. Take the following ad, for example:

Now, the unprepared job-seeker—the one who hasn't read *How to Be a Superhero*—might be inclined to overlook this opportunity, particularly if he or she a) isn't already a Magus Class hero, b) doesn't have three to five years of experience, or c) doesn't own or have access to an Orb of Shan'raa. But the savvy, well-informed job-hunter knows better. For him, qualifications are not the point. He will look at this listing and ask himself questions like: "What is this employer really looking for?" "What problems do they hope to solve by recruiting this type of hero?" and most importantly, "How can I fool them into offering me this job?" Here's how an EPM Class hero might respond to this listing:

March 3, 2004
15 Whistling Pines Terrace
Apex City, WA 95201

To Whom It May Concern,

I'm writing with regard to the listing that ran in today's *Apex City Herald* about a superhero position in one of your organization's Alternate Earth offices.

As a crimefighting professional with several years of valuable experience battling the forces of evil, I feel uniquely qualified to fulfill the requirements of this position. In addition to being a real go-getter who loves working with people, I have solid relationships with several prominent supervillains and have often found myself trapped in their various fiendish (and deadly!) mechanisms of death. I also enjoy saving the world from certain destruction, and in fact, just recently thwarted an insidious plot to import cheap electronic goods from Asia and pass the so-called savings on to unsuspecting consumers, a plan that could have had a catastrophic effect on global shopping patterns!

Though your listing specified a Magus Class hero, based on my familiarity with Earth 8's major supervillains (and your specific request regarding the Orb of Shan'raa), I suspect that any candidate who can project high-intensity beams of energy could ably fulfill the requirements of this position. As an EPM Class meta-human, I believe that my proven ability to absorb and project solar radiation — literally, the power to harness the vast destructive potential of the Sun itself! — would make me a valuable asset to your Earth 8 organization.

I welcome the opportunity to speak with you about this position, and I appreciate your consideration. If you'd like to set up a meeting, the best way to get in touch with me is by activating the Apex City Solar-Signal.

Kind regards,

Solaritrix
'Fiery Mistress of the Sun'

Notice how this hero was able to tailor her unique qualifications to fit the requirements of the position? Now let's take a look at what she's done with her résumé.

SOLARITRIX

15 Whistling Pines Terrace   The Solar-Signal
Apex City, WA 95201   solaritrix862@hotmail.com

OBJECTIVE
To contribute solar-sourced, directable-energy superpowers in a cutting-edge, justice-oriented environment

OVERVIEW OF QUALIFICATIONS
- Accomplished meta-human crusader and project manager. Works well in high-pressure, imminent-death situations. Able to balance and prioritize multiple threats.
- Resourceful crimefighter with proven skills in such areas as subduing, vanquishing, and masked intervention. Exceptionally adept at battling ice-wielding supervillains.
- Confirmed Magnitude E-6 directable-energy superpowers.

Familiar with EvilOrg 2.0, Digital HQ for Windows, and Filemaker Pro.

- Reliable problem-solver and team-player. Maintains focus on "big picture" issues—eager to sacrifice self for larger cause.

PROFESSIONAL EXPERIENCE
Apex City Office of Evil Management
Apex City, WA   1/02–Present
CONSULTANT

- Negotiated limited partnership with two other locally active superheroes that resulted in formation of the award-winning Century Squad
- Played key leadership role during the Century Squad's valiant repulse of an overly aggressive IRS investigation
- Spearheaded commission to investigate the long-range tax and employment implications of attacking and destroying DarkMind Laboratories, a local, privately held research consortium specializing in supplying positronic destabilizing technology to supervillains worldwide
- Played key leadership role in the development and implementation of the Century Squad's interactive Web site; site now averages 250 unique visitors per week

Justice, Inc.
New York City, NY   5/00–1/02
SENIOR HERO, OPERATIONS SECTION

- Designed and trained fellow heroes in new girder-flinging technique; increased crimefighting productivity by more than 28 percent

- Oversaw contracts with Starrion Labs for installation of new satellite-based evil-tracking system
- Supervised the defeat of or personally vanquished more than 20 supervillains during each year of employment
- Thwarted the Collective Farm-Raised Salmon's plot to turn ordinary people into scaly, water-breathing aqua-men

The Crime-Buster Corps
Rockville, MD   6/98–5/00
SIDEKICK
- Provided meaningful direction to senior staff by repeatedly getting captured and held hostage by various area supervillains
- Promoted pro-superhero policies through community outreach and puppet shows
- Established hostile relationships with leading henchmen, evil mistresses

The Crime-Buster Corps
Rockville, MD   2/95–6/98
INTERN/MASCOT
Enabled timely release of tension and stress through tired antics. Some typing and filing. Developed integrated marketing plan for roll-out of California office.

ACCOMPLISHMENTS
- *Who's Who Among Sidekicks,* 2000 Edition
- Graduate of the Phoenix Academy (Summer Session only)
- Honorable Mention, Super-Technology, Queens County Science Fair

Don't get discouraged if the first hundred or so résumés you send out are met with a negative response—or even no response at all! As I said at the beginning of this chapter, there are many opportunities out there, but today's employers are looking for something more than just the ability to alter your body's molecular density or shatter someone's brain with your sonic scream—they want superheroes who can think outside the box, who aren't afraid to take risks, and who won't use the team expense account to go drinking with friends and then claim it was "crimefighting related."

THE MYSTERY MEN

"The brave individuals known as 'crimefighters,' or sometimes, 'mystery men' (and informally catalogued as Crimefighter Class Heroes) have never been officially recognized by either the Valaxis Society or the government agency that followed it. In fact, though CCHs are active members of several prominent super-teams (as part of the 'don't ask, don't tell' policy), the group's application for formal admission into the ranks of super-heroes continues to be debated (for reasons that have never been satisfactorily explained) by the members of the BMHA's *Trijax Commission*.

"Little is known about the private lives of the early twentieth century mystery men (and most of what we do know comes from a series of interviews conducted between 1971 and 1973

by the historical meta-sociologist, Dr. Rex Rovin). Many of
them appear to have come from professions that either gave
them direct insight into the costs of the disintegrating social
order (for example, reporters, lawyers, and detectives); access to
new and unproven technologies (scientists, research professors,
and medical doctors); or a particular expertise with weapons and
vehicles (soldiers, test pilots, and spies). In some cases, crimefighters also came from the ranks of the upper class (they were
known, officially, as 'millionaire playboys' or 'wealthy industrial-
ists'), and were able to draw upon substantial personal fortunes
to help support their vigilante activities.*

"In the years before World War II, newspapers such as the
Daily Globe in New York, the *Sun-Times* in Chicago, and the
Herald-Tribune in Apex City all began to run stories about bank
robberies thwarted, hostages rescued, and smuggling rings
smashed, not by the police, the feds, or even superheroes, but
rather by shadowy, mysterious figures. For example, there was
Mister Midnight, who subdued his foes using 'reverse-blindness
bombs,' a 'tri-radio belt,' and his special hypno-stun ray; *Lady
Lariat* (later revealed to have been the rodeo performer, Belle
Barnes) who would bewitch criminals with her great beauty before capturing them with her special elasti-steel lasso; *Arrowsmith*,
who fought crime with the help of the Archermobile, his combination flying car/submarine, and his quiver of trick crimefighting

---

*While money was not a prerequisite to becoming a mystery man in the early 1900s, as
several enterprising but solidly middle-class crimefighters demonstrated, it became something of an absolute necessity as the century wore on and powerful supervillains and
megalomaniacs replaced the gangsters and saboteurs of the 1920s, '30s, and '40s.

arrows; and even groups like the *Twelve Angry Men*, each one a crack shot who carried a uniquely modified rifle or machine gun.

"With World War II came a new sort of crimefighter. Focused on battling saboteurs, spies, and Axis super-soldiers, these heroes traded the simple trenchcoat and black mask of the earlier generation for flight suits, star-spangled uniforms, and increasingly silly names. Fighting the war at home, for example, were heroes like *Dickie Dare, Ace Test Pilot*, as well as the *Pint-Size Commandos*; overseas, the *Masked Mariner*, and *Hank Hannigan and his American Eagles* battled the Axis powers from the sea and air. Finally, there was *Robot Abe Lincoln*, a sophisticated, super-secret android, whose creator, Professor U. S. Jones, was killed by a Nazi spy before he could begin mass production. This radium-powered version of the Great Emancipator played a significant role in several campaigns before being scrapped in favor of the more advanced *Robot Grover Cleveland*.

"The postwar years were witness to an alarming rise of powerful supervillains and nihilistic madmen who were anxious to move beyond armed car robbery and diamond smuggling, and into areas such as world domination and apocalypse. In response to these threats, new crimefighters have emerged. Though the days of taking down meta-criminals armed with only a squared jaw, a "frictionless gun," and a gut-full of determination are over, the spirit of the crimefighter lives on in the exploits of heroes like the *Night Watchman*, a mysterious figure who uses his prohibitively expensive arsenal of weapons, gadgets, and vehicles (including a heli-tank and stealth-sub) to keep Metro City safe; *Citadel*, who fights evil with the help of his powerful, state-of-the-art battlesuit; and *Wetworx*, a vengeful, reasonably unstable ex-Special Forces soldier who uses military technology and tactics to wage a brutal war on the criminal underworld."—from *"We Are Legion": The Mark of the Mystery Men,* by Jessica Paris

On the Other Hand, Maybe You're Evil

Though we may not even realize it, from the moment we acquire our superpowers we find ourselves bombarded by messages from family, friends, mentors, and various godlike beings. Everyone seems to have their own idea about who we should be, how we should act, and even why we should fight. Before long it can start to feel like everyone just wants us to use our powers for good.

Of course, most of us have no problem with this. The majority of meta-humans naturally embrace concepts such as truth, justice, and Christmas. However, for some heroes, doing the right thing can feel, well, *wrong*. They may be confused by the sudden urge to help, not hinder, a villain's diabolical plot. They may have trouble understanding why it's wrong to hold a city hostage with a molecular transmogrifying ray. And they may even find themselves becoming physically aroused at the mere mention of world domination.

Inevitably, these heroes will start asking themselves the question: "Am I evil?" Despite what you may have heard, the only reliable way to answer this question is through the following self-assessment protocol, originally developed by Marco Crisafulli and Micah France as part of *Project Q*. Be sure to set aside at least thirty minutes in order to complete all the questions.

PART 1

1. **I sometimes feel confused or uncertain when people talk about doing the "right" thing.**

   ☐ Strongly disagree   ☐ Somewhat disagree   ☐ No opinion
   ☐ Somewhat agree   ☐ Strongly agree

2. **I am always surprised or even somewhat disappointed when movies or books have a happy ending.**

   ☐ Strongly disagree   ☐ Somewhat disagree   ☐ No opinion
   ☐ Somewhat agree   ☐ Strongly agree

3. **I often feel the urge to take over the world.**

   ☐ Strongly disagree   ☐ Somewhat disagree   ☐ No opinion
   ☐ Somewhat agree   ☐ Strongly agree

4. **I feel strangely anxious whenever I hear others describe the warm glow they get from saving lives and thwarting evil.**

   ☐ Strongly disagree   ☐ Somewhat disagree   ☐ No opinion
   ☐ Somewhat agree   ☐ Strongly agree

5. **I frequently experience the overpowering urge to hold my own sidekick hostage.**

   ☐ Strongly disagree   ☐ Somewhat disagree   ☐ No opinion
   ☐ Somewhat agree   ☐ Strongly agree

6. **Fire is pretty.**

☐ Strongly disagree   ☐ Somewhat disagree   ☐ No opinion
☐ Somewhat agree   ☐ Strongly agree

7. **I often fantasize about unleashing some kind of deadly plague on civilian populations.**

☐ Strongly disagree   ☐ Somewhat disagree   ☐ No opinion
☐ Somewhat agree   ☐ Strongly agree

8. **I'm not exactly sure what a "conscience" is.**

☐ Strongly disagree   ☐ Somewhat disagree   ☐ No opinion
☐ Somewhat agree   ☐ Strongly agree

9. **I occasionally wonder if I'm wasting my potential by trying to thwart evil instead of enabling it.**

☐ Strongly disagree   ☐ Somewhat disagree   ☐ No opinion
☐ Somewhat agree   ☐ Strongly agree

10. **I sometimes find myself admiring supervillains' cunning schemes and thinking of how I could improve on them.**

☐ Strongly disagree   ☐ Somewhat disagree   ☐ No opinion
☐ Somewhat agree   ☐ Strongly agree

11. **I frequently find myself writing my supervillain name over and over.**

☐ Strongly disagree   ☐ Somewhat disagree   ☐ No opinion
☐ Somewhat agree   ☐ Strongly agree

12. **I get frustrated when I see supervillains not giving their evil plans the time and attention that they deserve.**

☐ Strongly disagree   ☐ Somewhat disagree   ☐ No opinion
☐ Somewhat agree   ☐ Strongly agree

EVALUATING YOUR SCORE

To calculate your score, assign each of your answers a numerical equivalent. At the end of the quiz, you'll add your score from Part 1 to your score from Part 2 to find your evil-doing potential.

Strongly agree = 5; Somewhat agree = 4; No opinion = 3; Somewhat disagree = 2; Strongly disagree = 1

PART 2
Evil Math Skills Assessment:

13. Apex City is holding a parade to celebrate the city's founding. Ten thousand people are expected to attend. If each of your cybernetic dinosaurs can kill twenty people, how many cybernetic dinosaurs will you need in order to kill all the attendees?

    a) 406
    b) 129
    c) 37
    d) 500

14. You have captured your do-gooder nemesis and suspended him 5 meters above a tank of genetically enhanced piranhas. The electric winch you're using to lower him into the tank has a top speed of 1.3 meters per minute. At that rate, how

much time do you have in which to reveal the inner work-
ings of your master plan?
a) 2 minutes, 45 seconds
b) 3 minutes, 4 seconds
c) 1 minute, 58 seconds
d) Need more information

15. How big would the circumference of your doom-bomb's
perpetual devastation blast need to be in order to destroy
your archenemy's secret headquarters?

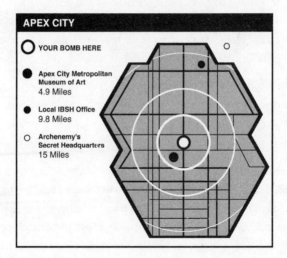

a) 31 miles
b) 62 miles
c) 94 miles
d) Not applicable; even if he survived the blast, the radiation cloud would surely kill him

Evil Verbal Skills Assessment:

16. *Maim* is to *bludgeon* as . . .
    a) *Henchman* is to *cretin*
    b) *Destroy* is to *incinerate*
    c) *Sidekick* is to *bait*
    d) *Freeze ray* is to *mind-control device*

17. "Now all I need is a _____ and my _____
    will be complete!"
    a) laser-guided dirigible . . . evil air armada
    b) fragment of eternium . . . black-hole gun
    c) nonconsenting test subject . . . diabolical experiment
    d) freeze-dried superhero . . . grotesque menagerie of do-
       gooders

Directions: Answer the questions below based on the information in the accompanying passage.

To Whom It May Concern,

As you may have guessed, the rare synthetic element I stole during my
daring infiltration of the N.O.V.A. Tech complex last week has allowed
me to finish work on my latest masterpiece of evil, the destabilization
field generator. In its current form, this powerful device enables me to
disrupt the inner-ear balance of anyone within a fifty-mile radius. Impressive as that is, it's but a taste of the incapacitating nausea and
dizziness to come. Once I patch into the Sparta satellite system, the entire planet will fall beneath my queasily enfeebling tyranny! If you wish
to avoid the vomit-drenched fate of Utica, NY, then you, the assembled

leaders of the world's nations, must deliver to me $500 billion worth of
uncut diamonds by tomorrow at midnight!
Sincerely,
The Yellow Claw

18. In the first sentence, why does the author mention the
    N.O.V.A. Tech company?
    a) To establish his credibility
    b) To provide them with some free publicity
    c) To credit them with irresponsibly developing a wide ar-
       ray of potentially deadly products
    d) To allude to the important role that scientific innova-
       tion plays in our lives

19. According to the author, what exactly will the "destabiliza-
    tion field generator" do?
    a) Enable companies to double their productivity
    b) Help children everywhere learn to read
    c) Turn milk chocolatey
    d) Scramble our delicate inner-ear coils and reduce us to
       trembling, vomit-soaked invalids

20. In the closing sentence, the author cautions that something
    must be delivered to him before midnight tomorrow. That
    something is:
    a) $500 billion in galactic credits
    b) $500 billion in pilfered monkey glands
    c) $500 billion in uncut diamonds
    d) $500 billion in quarters, dimes, and nickels

Evaluating Your Score

To calculate your score, first assign each of your answers a numerical equivalent:

a) = 1; b) = 2; c) = 3; d) = 4

Now, add up your scores from both parts of the quiz and find your evil-doing potential below:

92–73: You are quite possibly the Antichrist.

72–52: You are a cruel blight upon this world.

51–32: You frequently have impure thoughts regarding luncheon meat.

31–0: Congratulations! You are officially *not* evil!.*

WHAT TO EXPECT WHEN "COMING OUT" TO YOUR TEAMMATES

When revealing your evil nature to the other members of your superheroic team, league, legion, or even to your sidekick, it's important to remember that, deep down, your colleagues and supervisors really do just want what's best for you (the sentimental fools!). For this reason alone, coming out is well worth your while, as you'll get a front-row seat to amusingly pathetic hijinks like:

---

*Caution: This should not be construed as a guarantee of continuing non-evil status.

- Crying, sobbing, uncontrollable gnashing of teeth
- Accusing you of doing this "to hurt them" (a particularly satisfying response, since it serves both your need for emotional honesty as well as your craving for pain!)
- Guilt: "Did *we* make you evil? Did we somehow drive you to this?"
- Insisting that evil is a choice: "Well, I don't see why you can't just *stop* being evil."
- Promising to help you change back into being good: "There must be places that can help people like you. Please, let us try. We'll find a good therapist, we'll help you change. And if that doesn't work, we can always have you banished to the Shadow Zone."

Remember, the decision to come out is never one you should make lightly. Also keep in mind that by coming out, you'll most likely be sacrificing the element of surprise, and along with it the delicious satisfaction of seeing your teammates' expressions as you gleefully stab them in their stupidly unsuspecting backs.

> "People fear what they don't understand—except for evil, which they understand fairly well and yet fear diligently."   —The Mucus Master

A Guide to Revealing Your Evil Nature

As you can see by the range of possible responses, coming out is never easy, no matter how enlightened your teammates may think they are. And while there's no way to completely avoid the discomfort and awkwardness of such moments, I hope that the following standardized coming-out template will take some of the uncertainty out of the process and make it all seem a little less painful (for you, at least).

STEP ONE: ESTABLISH AN UPBEAT TONE

Some people, including even some supervillains who should know better, will tell you that any admission of evil should be counterbalanced by a warning to your listeners that you're about to tell them something horrible to which they must promise to respond calmly. The idea behind this strategy is to overprepare your audience to the point where they'll regard any news not directly related to the apocalypse as a bit of a relief.

While this approach can work, I don't like to use it because right from the get-go it communicates one thing, which is: you're here to tell them something *bad*. In the long run, I think it's far healthier for everyone involved if you start out on a positive note. Therefore, don't just confess that you're evil—proclaim it! Admit your evilness with the same smug humility you might use to discuss the merits of a particularly fine merlot. The unfathomable disconnect between your tone and message should leave your listeners stunned and temporarily unable to respond. Seize this opportunity to smirk condescendingly.

STEP TWO:
APPEAR TO GIVE A SHIT

Once the temporarily incapacitating effects of your announcement
wear off, your former colleagues
will begin to react. While they may
cry, plead, or order you to "get the
hell out of this secret headquarters

> **HELPFUL HINT ALERT!**
> Being evil is still against the
> law in many states. Check
> with your local BMHA office
> for an update on your legal
> status.

right now and never come back," all you need do is pretend to
actually care. In other words: Nod your head every now and
then. Repeat what was just said or simply let out a thoughtful
"Hmmm" or "I see." This will fool them into thinking that they
can still "reach you" or some such horseshit, allowing you to re-
tain the upper hand while they wallow in their delusions. Of
course, don't feel compelled to *actually* listen to what they're
saying. If their pathetic yammering grows unbearable (as it almost certainly will), you may choose to pass the time by imag-
ining them all suffering horribly in a deathtrap of your own
design. (Be careful, however, not to let on that you're indulging
in an evil daydream. Even the slightest curl of a malicious smile
could give you away!)

STEP THREE: UNLEASH THE FULL POWER OF YOUR DARK SIDE
Step Three is really the only possible reason why anyone would
endure the agony of Steps One and Two. But by indulging your
former teammates' pathetic need to slavishly bare their souls,
talk about their feelings, and submit feeble appeals to the shriv-
eled nerve endings of your "better nature," you've thrown them

LET'S MEET . . . COLLECTIVE FARM-RAISED SALMON!
"Coming to us courtesy of yet another irresponsible Cold War experiment," the Collective Farm-Raised Salmon was "spawned in a secret KGB lab somewhere in the Urals" and reared on a "diet of high-intensity radiation, Marxist ideology, and pink food coloring." The "only survivor" of the "KGB's infamous 'Room Seven,'" the Collective Farm-Raised Salmon was known during the Cold War as "Weapon N," and is believed to be behind "the mysterious beachings of several MI-6-affiliated pilot whales." When "the Soviet Union collapsed, Weapon N disappeared," later resurfacing as the Collective Farm-Raised Salmon. With his "freakish legs," "opposable fins," "razor-sharp projectile scales," and "uncanny grasp of Leninist doctrine," the Salmon is determined to "liberate his aquatic brethren from the bottom-dragging oppressions of fish-stick-scarfing capitalists," particularly the "hated Gorton Fisherman and his ilk." "Aquatic heroes, be warned," the Collective Farm-Raised Salmon "has already launched repeated and deadly attacks" on "the surface-dwellers' navies, coastal cities, and harbor taxis."—from *Mister Mental's Survey of Supervillains,* 2003 edition

hopelessly off their game. By duping them into asking probing, heartfelt questions like, "How can we convince you that you're not evil, just confused?" when the only question they should be asking is "Where the heck is my ion cannon?" you've skillfully outmaneuvered them. Because what they don't get—what they *can't* get, not being evil themselves—is that any moment not spent imprisoning, torturing, or massacring them is spent in preparation for one or all of those activities. So push the secret button that will unseal the blast doors and admit your lurking hordes; activate the containment domes that will drop down over these mewling do-gooders and render them helpless; set the self-destruct timer and make your getaway in their own escape pod—you've earned it!

"EVIL IS A CAPTURED SIDEKICK":
A POEM BY MADAM MAYHEM

Evil is receiving the ransom in your Swiss bank account
And wiping out Portland anyway.
Evil is saying, "Let's get together for lunch," and then
Never, ever calling.
Evil is pretending that a movie shot in Toronto
Is actually taking place in New York.
Evil is any device with a "Kill" setting.
Evil is drinking blood—
Not because you have to,
But because you like the taste.
But most of all,
Evil is never having to say
You're sorry.

CRAFTING AN EVIL BUSINESS PLAN

While it would be great if all there was to being a supervillain was slaughtering your former colleagues and laying waste to the charming bedroom communities of Detroit, the truth is that today's supervillain faces a multitude of daunting challenges. Skyrocketing labor costs and the scarcity of the rare elements (such as eternium) that power many of our modern doomsday machines have thwarted almost as many plans as superheroic meddling. Lately, however, some enterprising supervillains have sought inspiration from an unlikely source: the world of business.

Though at first the idea of turning to the *Harvard Business Review* for dastardly insights, as opposed to the venerable *Journal of Misanthropy,* may seem ludicrous, upon closer examination it starts to make sense—particularly when you look at it over the long term. Consider the masterpieces of evil that multinational corporations have been able to achieve—for example, the Savings & Loan Crisis, the *Exxon Valdez,* Enron—and then compare them against a century's worth of promising but ultimately unrealized or foiled master plans and villainous machinations: clearly, the evil community has a lot to learn from the business world.

Evil Business Plans Made Easy

Nowhere else has the business world's influence been felt more strongly than in the planning of the magnificently evil schemes that are the hallmark of all great supervillains. With such master plans growing ever more complex, there is no longer room for the villain who claims to have it all laid out in his freakishly large, vein-pulsing head. Rarer still is the criminal mastermind or megalomaniacal industrialist who can afford today's premium weapons systems, such as tractor beams or giant, hero-smashing robots. Given the risks inherent in trying to take over the world, today's evil investors want to see a disciplined evil business plan before they'll agree to advance you enough money to finish that mind-control ray.

LET'S MEET . . . DOCTOR OMINOUS!

"If you're tired of costumed cat burglars and glorified gangsters," then Doctor Ominous "might be just what the power-crazed mad scientist ordered." The bastard son of "the devious Nazi occultist and petting-zoo magnate, Rufus Von Ominous," young Heinrich grew up "determined to erase the stain his father had left on the family name." One night, while "working late in the dungeon laboratory of the Von Ominous ancestral castle," "a slight miscalculation" by the young scientist "triggered a violent chain reaction." Heinrich became "trapped in a furious inferno of leaping flames and collapsing ceiling joists." Fortunately, the lab's sprinkler system "helped contain the fire" and "no serious damage was done" except that the "carpets had to be replaced." After realizing that "non-evil scientific research was a dead-end,

> career-wise," Heinrich "decided to re-stain the family name, becoming *Doctor Ominous*." "If you're lucky," he'll attempt to use his "brain-disorganizing gun or death-ray," on you, but in any event "don't finish him off until you've seen his one-of-a-kind hypno-hovercar!"   —from *Mister Mental's Survey of Supervillains,* 2003 edition

Don't let the name intimidate you, however. An evil business plan is simply a document that describes your latest chillingly malevolent enterprise and what you will need in order to make it a reality. Read on to discover a helpful brainstorming exercise I've included to get you thinking about evil plans, as well as a sample evil business plan you can consult in case you get stuck.

> "Always test your doomsday device on something— Cleveland, for instance—before trying to use it to hold the world hostage. Nothing kills an evil plan like not being able to vaporize the United Nations when you said you would."   —The Planetmaster

EVIL BRAINSTORMING TOOL

The point of this exercise is to get your vindictive juices flowing. There are no right or wrong answers; rather, just unshackle your sinister nature and let it rip. Push yourself to see how many different evil plans you can think of. Also, keep in mind that while this exercise is structured in the form of an ultimatum, such as the kind you might deliver to a local Rotary Club or the president of France, you should refrain from using this as a model for any actual ultimatums you deliver, since it might make you sound "canned."

"Greetings, _____. You may call me _____.
              noun   name and/or title

Possible nouns include:

Earthlings	Grandma
Surface-dwellers	Ladies and gentlemen of the jury
Meat-bags	Citizens of Apex City
Wal-Mart shoppers	Registered voters

"As you may be aware, my _____ _____ are
                                   adj/adverb   evil noun

Possible adj/adv include: *Possible evil nouns include:*

stylish	hordes
merciless	demons
cryptic	henchmen
remorseless	zombies
relentless	mutants
aching	henchwomen
whimsical	werewolves
shuffling	child stars
wheezing	evil twins
sobbing	baristas
bloodthirsty	

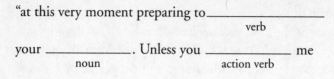

"at this very moment preparing to _____
                                            verb

your _____. Unless you _____ me
              noun   action verb

Possible verbs include: *Possible nouns include:* *Possible action verbs include:*

destroy   city   pay

vaporize   nation   grant

kick   loose confederation   show

taunt   of states   send

ridicule   original 13 colonies   wire

melt   theme park   give

smash   monorail system   offer

crush   local shopping mall   feed

wrinkle   lawn

mutilate   collection of Pez

renovate   dispensers

                            porno stash

                            foot/tonsils/crotch

"_____ _____
          number   noun

by _____, I will have no choice but
        date/time

Possible nouns include:

Rubles

Uncut diamonds

Rubles

Wampum

Shiny objects

Signed editions of Joe Cocker's *Ultimate Collection* CD

Secret passwords

"to unleash the torrent of devastation I referred to earlier. And I advise you not to waste your precious time attempting to contact _____. As you can see, he/she is '_____'
            your nemesis   hilarious pun

Possible hilarious puns include:

A little tied up

Feeling under the weather

Having trouble getting away

Drowning in paperwork

Dead on his/her feet

Being eaten alive by marmots

Trapped inside a diabolical funhouse of death

Growing ever-weaker as the virus takes effect

Getting torn to pieces by rabid monkey-sharks

Strapped to a table watching a giant laser scorch his crotch

Deceased

"at the moment! _____

" _____

" _____

" _____

"_____

"_____!!!!!!"
     insane laughter (recommended)

Possible expressions of inappropriate mirth include:
     Ha-ha-ha-ha-ha-ha-ha-ha-ha-ha-ha-ha
     Bwa-ha-ha-ha-ha-ha-ha-ha-ha-ha
     Ha-ha-ha-ha-ha-(snort)uh-huh-huh-ha-ha
     Also:
     Evil chortling
     Dreadful snickering
     Unfortunate giggling
     Deadly guffawing
     Offensive snorting
     Ominous chuckling
     Sinister retching
     A kind of unsettling wheezing sound

AN EXAMPLE OF AN EVIL BUSINESS PLAN
The following master plan was recognized as one of the year's
most devious at the recent Northeastern Regional Evil Business
Plan competition, which was held at the Ithaca Marriott and
sponsored jointly by Cornell University's Johnson School of
Management and Kellogg Brown & Root. An excellent example of how the entrepreneurial spirit and the killer instinct com-

plement each other, you would do well to study it carefully. Who knows, maybe next year your plan will take home the cherished Ken Lay Award! (Note: If you find that you can't summarize your evil intentions in this format, chances are you haven't totally thought things through.)

HATE-U

SUMMARY OF EVIL VISION

The Horde of Amalgamated Terror-Mongers and Evil-Doers Unlimited (HATE-U) is dedicated to developing innovative doomsday products and diabolical master plans for the villainous consumer. HATE-U is seeking to raise $6.2 trillion from evil investors in order to facilitate the development, testing, and catastrophic deployment of a next-generation, geocidal energy weapon (the Bitterbork Anti-Existence Machine, or AEM) with several apocalyptic applications. The ideal investor brings complementary industry or evil-doing experience and a passion for grinding the planet into dust beneath his/her iron heel.

EVIL OBJECTIVES

The typical evil household purchases seven doomsday devices a year. However, our surveys suggest that most supervillains would be willing to increase their doomsday device outlays by *more than 50 percent* if they felt that these additional devices would add significant ROE (return on evil) to their abominable activities. Judging by the early promise of our groundbreaking AEM (patent pending), we here at HATE-U feel uniquely positioned to capture a substantial portion of this rapidly growing market.

- Forge strategic alliances with world's leading criminal masterminds and superpowered warlords in order to provide credibility and established channels of distribution
- License the underlying technology to evil alien races and other-dimensional warrior-kings
- Establish a strong presence in the evil marketplace
- Bring world to its knees

THE BITTERBORK AEM:
A MASTERPIECE OF TWISTED INGENUITY

The AEM offers several key competitive advantages over conventional means of administering widespread pain and suffering, thanks to its relative affordability, ease of use, and catastrophic ability to disrupt the balance of the Earth's various geo-forces. Unlike other so-called global threats, the Bitterbork AEM enables its user to oppress mankind on a truly international scale, thanks to its sub-orbital delivery platform and cutting-edge stealth capabilities. No other doomsday device offers such flexibility and destructive power right out of the box. Also, its atomic core has been thoroughly tested and is rated for at least eighteen hours of constant use (enough to bring the world under your cruel dominion at least *twice*).

- Delivers a genuinely apocalyptic experience with every use
- Automated, single-source delivery removes the need for complex network of bombs, elaborate missile-hijacking

plots, or costly human/mutant assets such as spies, assassins, or henchpeople
- Produces a variety of cataclysmic scenarios, including tidal waves, earthquakes, volcanic eruptions, hurricanes, tornadoes, and droughts up to ten times (10x) faster than comparable devices
- Low maintenance requirements result in significantly reduced operating expenses

CHOOSING THE RIGHT TIME
TO REVEAL YOUR DIABOLICAL PLOT

Writing a dynamite evil business plan is one thing, but executing it requires an entirely different evil skill-set. One common misunderstanding regarding secret plans is the point at which you should reveal the finely tuned meshing of your scheme's gears, pulleys, and levers to your irritatingly noble and well behaved nemesis. In fact, I've even had people ask me the question: "Why reveal your plans at all? Wouldn't it be more expedient to just *kill* your do-gooder archenemy as soon as you get the chance?"

Well, gosh, I guess it would. And while you're at it, why not tamper with the brakes of his crimefighting-mobile? Or take all the cash from that bank job and put it into a nice mix of stocks and bonds? Look, if being a supervillain were only about *winning,* this would be a cake gig. But plotting to destroy the world is about more than pain and suffering—it's about self-actualization. It's about reaching your full potential as an evil-doer. Supervillains, like anyone else, crave recognition, and there's no sweeter form of acknowledgment than that look on a superhero's face when he realizes that your finger's on the button, and you're just mad enough to push it.

The following handy flow chart should help you decide if it's the right time to offer your archnemesis a little glimpse into the insidious machinations of your fevered brain.

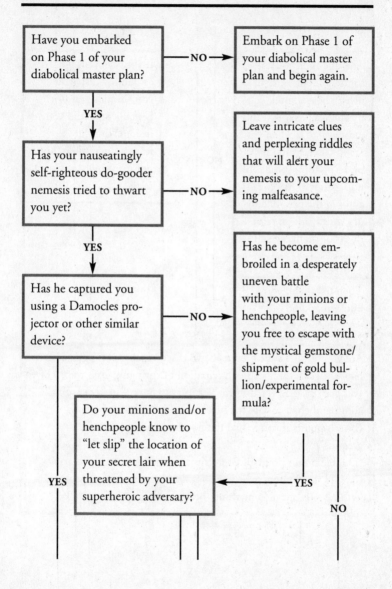

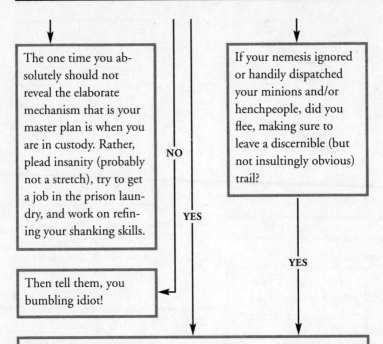

The one time you absolutely should not reveal the elaborate mechanism that is your master plan is when you are in custody. Rather, plead insanity (probably not a stretch), try to get a job in the prison laundry, and work on refining your shanking skills.

NO

If your nemesis ignored or handily dispatched your minions and/or henchpeople, did you flee, making sure to leave a discernible (but not insultingly obvious) trail?

YES

YES

Then tell them, you bumbling idiot!

Are you lurking stealthily inside your secret lair, rubbing your hands together in gleeful anticipation of springing your trap? Have you perhaps placed a dummy version of yourself in your special command chair to lure the hero into your hide-out?
(Bonus points if you've had the foresight to tape record a greeting!)
(Double bonus points if you wait until the moment the hero touches the dummy, whereupon it flops over and maybe some stuffing falls out or something, before springing your trap!!)

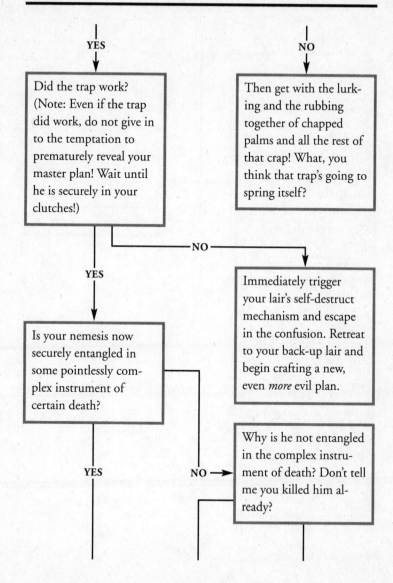

YES

Did the trap work?
(Note: Even if the trap
did work, do not give in
to the temptation to
prematurely reveal your
master plan! Wait until
he is securely in your
clutches!)

NO

Then get with the lurk-
ing and the rubbing
together of chapped
palms and all the rest of
that crap! What, you
think that trap's going to
spring itself?

NO

YES

Is your nemesis now
securely entangled in
some pointlessly com-
plex instrument of
certain death?

Immediately trigger
your lair's self-destruct
mechanism and escape
in the confusion. Retreat
to your back-up lair and
begin crafting a new,
even *more* evil plan.

YES

NO

Why is he not entangled
in the complex instru-
ment of death? Don't tell
me you killed him al-
ready?

This is the moment you've been waiting for! Now you may regale your helpless captive with all the myriad and no doubt fascinating details behind your mad scheme. The early obstacles, the creative roadblocks, the fights between team members, the late night pizza-and-Red-Bull blitzes, the missed deadlines, the laughter and the tears. Take a moment to bask in your adversary's horror (and grudging admiration), and then leave to carry out the final phase of your plan while your device of death puts an end to this meddlesome hero once and for all.

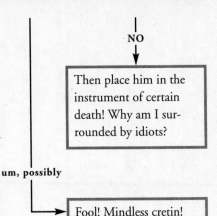

NO

Then place him in the instrument of certain death! Why am I surrounded by idiots?

um, possibly

Fool! Mindless cretin!

Epilogue

I believe it was Sixty-Minute Samson who said, "With great power come tax breaks, and with moderate power come unavoidable community obligations and a better parking space, while with minimal power comes a book of valuable coupons redeemable at local shops." And though much of what that legendary hero said after his defeat at the hands of *Tyranno* is either unsuitable for publication or simply unintelligible, he did manage to get it right that one last time. Nothing else, I think, sums up the superheroic experience quite so well.

You've come a long way over the course of this book. You've learned how to hone your superpowers, select an appropriate secret headquarters, and design a costume that strikes fear into the hearts of evil-doers everywhere (but can be washed with like colors). And yet, one very important lesson still remains.

You may have already heard other superheroes talk about the *Meridian Codex*. This codex, or statement of our heroic principles, isn't like the other things we've covered in this book. It's not something that you memorize or have printed on a bumper sticker for easy reference. Rather, the codex is something that exists in the heart of every true hero. Sure, the words may differ from person to person. And okay, sometimes the spelling might be a little off. But the fundamental message is always the same. A true hero must:

Help the helpless.

Protect the powerless.

And always, always do the right thing.

About the Author

Doctor Metropolis (shown here in his pre–Phantom Wars costume) has been serving as a consultant to the superpowered community for more than twenty years. Drawing on his own experiences as a costumed crusader in addition to what he's learned while helping his clients, Doctor Metropolis is a unique authority on the subject of meta-human coaching and professional development. He's appeared on *Oprah, Montel,* and *Live with Go-Girl and Ms. Manta!* A longtime resident of Apex City, he lives in a tastefully decorated secret headquarters beneath Union Park with his sidekick and their two cats, Mr. Pooh and Ticklesticks. Though Doctor Metropolis has several superpowers, the one he values most is "the power to help others reach their full potential." You can e-mail him at drmetropolis84@ yahoo.com.

About the Illustrator

Before opening his creative studio, Luis Roca worked for MTV Networks as a senior graphic designer. He has won a number of awards, including the Broadcast Designer's Award in 2001, 2002, and 2003, and his work has been featured in *Creative* magazine. He currently resides in the New York area with his wife and two finches. You can contact Luis at luis@thepopularmovement.com.